UNIVERSITY OF CAMBRIDGE

INSTITUTE OF CRIMINOLOGY

CRIMINOLOGICAL IMPLICATIONS
OF
CHROMOSOME ABNORMALITIES

Papers presented to the

Cropwood Round - Table Conference

December 1969

edited by

D.J. West

Lecturer in Criminology

and Fellow of Darwin College

Cambridge , 1969

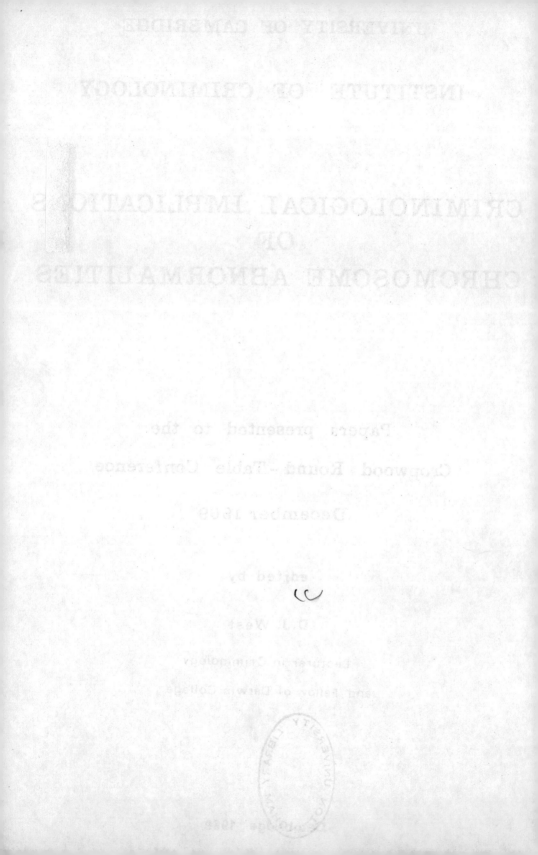

CONTENTS

Foreword   Page
    L. RADZINOWICZ   5

Editor's Preface
    D.J. WEST   7

Notice   8

Criminological Implications of Sex Chromosome Abnormalities:
  A Review
    T.K. MACLACHLAN   9

An Investigation of a Group of XYY Prisoners
    A.W. GRIFFITHS *et al*   32

Chromosome Studies in Remand Home and Prison Populations
    E.T.O. SLATER, J. KAHN, W.I. CARTER and N. DERNLEY   44

The Family and Behavioral History of Patients with Chromosome
  Abnormality in the Special Hospitals of Rampton and Moss Side
    M.D. CASEY   49

Patients with Chromosome Abnormalities in Rampton Hospital:
  A Report
    D.R.K. STREET and R.A. WATSON   61

E.E.G. Findings in Male Patients with Sex Chromsome Abnormalities
  in a Security Prison
    E.W. POOLE   68

Further Studies of 47XYY Constitution in Prepubertal Child
    J. COWIE   87

Chromosome Abnormality and Legal Accountability
    J.E. HALL WILLIAMS   100

Bibliography   108

LIST OF PARTICIPANTS

Dr. R.P. Brittain, Forensic Psychiatric Clinic, Woodside Crescent, Glasgow.

Dr. M.D. Casey, Lecturer in Human Genetics, Sheffield.

Dr. John Cowie, Consultant Psychiatrist, Putney, London.

Dr. A.W. Griffiths, Medical Officer, The Hospital, H.M. Prison, Wandsworth.

Mr. J.E. Hall Williams, Reader in Criminology in the University of London, The London School of Economics.

Dr. H. Hunter, Medical Superintendent, Balderton Hospital, Newark.

Dr. T.K. Maclachlan, Child Guidance Service, Worcester.

Dr. P.G. McGrath, Physician Superintendent, Broadmoor Hospital.

Dr. I.G.W. Pickering, Prison Department, Home Office.

Dr. E.W. Poole, E.E.G. Department, The Churchill Hospital, Oxford.

Dr. E. Slater, Department of Psychiatry, Denmark Hill, London.

Dr. D.R.K. Street, Medical Superintendent, Rampton Hospital, Retford.

Dr. T.G. Tennent, Special Hospitals Research Unit, Broadmoor Hospital.

Dr. D.J. West, Lecturer in Criminology, Institute of Criminology.

Dr. P.B. Whatmore, Consultant Psychiatrist, H.M. Prison, Perth.

Foreword by the Director of the Institute

This most recent of the activities of the Institute has been made possible by the interest of a philanthropist, who has given generous financial support to launch a series of short-term fellowships and conferences. These are to be known as <u>Cropwood Fellowships</u> and <u>Cropwood Conferences</u>.

Their purpose is to enable the people who do the work in the administration of the criminal law and the treatment of offenders to spend time at the Institute, individually or in groups, considering problems that face them in their day-to-day responsibilities.

The Fellowships and Conferences are differently organised, but they have the common thread of promoting the interchange of knowledge, ideas and experience between academics, administrators and practitioners. By publication and other means we shall endeavour to ensure that the benefit derived from these contacts and studies will extend beyond the circle of those who are initially drawn into them.

We are now publishing the working documents of the Fourth Cropwood Conference, which was held at the Institute in December 1969. It is hoped that this collection of papers, and the accompanying bibliography, will be of help to those involved in what is a new and exciting field of criminological endeavour - the investigation of the association between deviant behaviour and chromosome abnormalities.

I should like to thank all the participants, and especially those who contributed papers, for their ready cooperation.

LEON RADZINOWICZ

Institute of Criminology,
Cambridge, April 1970.

Editor's Preface

Explanations of criminality in terms of inborn defects of the individual have a long tradition in criminology, extending back to Lombroso and beyond. They have also considerable popular appeal, perhaps because it is comforting to stigmatise rule-breakers as personally inadequate. Certainly the idea that chromosome anomalies may be a cause of aggressive criminality has been taken up enthusiastically by the press and in public discussions. A collection of expert papers on the topic may therefore be welcomed, both as a timely corrective to premature conclusions, and as a stimulus to further interest in what is a complex and still largely unexplored area of knowledge.

Recent spectacular advances in molecular biology and genetics have opened up new avenues of exploration which must lead to a rapid expansion of knowledge of the nature and mechanism of inherited abnormalities. Hitherto, clinical interest has centred upon gross and easily recognised physical abnormalities, but now that micropathology serves to identify more subtle forms of disturbance, it becomes possible to trace to genetic causes a wider range of disorders. The discovery of an unusually high incidence of double Y chromosome males in special hospitals and in prisons has had a double impact on criminology. First, the anomaly is not necessarily associated with mental subnormality, and the only manifest physical peculiarity common to a high proportion of cases is unusual tallness. It seems, therefore, that in the double Y cases one has an identifiable and gross genetic anomaly that produces minimal, or at least unobtrusive, physical disorder, but quite gross disturbance of behaviour. From the theoretical standpoint, this discovery opens the door to the possibility that, even in the absence of manifest neurological impairment, behaviour disturbances may have genetic rather than environmental determinants.

The second reason for criminological interest in the XYY cases is the suggestion that the associated behavioural disturbance tends to be of a specifically violent, or at least antisocial, character. This suggestion stems from the relatively high incidence among criminal populations in institutions, and from the occasional detection of the anomaly among men on trial for murder, but until it is known how many cases survive unnoticed among the normal community it is open to speculation in what proportion of XYY cases antisocial behaviour is a necessary or unavoidable outcome. As the papers which follow will show, the characteristics attributed to XYY males vary considerably according to the way the sample under examination is selected.

Since the Y chromosome mediates the development of male primary ·and secondary sexual characteristics, it is tempting to imagine that the possession of a double dose of Y chromosome will lead to super masculinity. In fact some of the alleged XYY attributes (tallness, aggressiveness, and criminality) are male-linked characteristics, but this is probably a considerable over-simplification. There is no evidence that XYY males are unusually potent or fertile heterosexuals; rather the reverse, bachelorhood, social isolation, and sexual deviation being mentioned rather often in published case studies.

At first sight the practical importance of chromosomal abnormalities in forensic work may seem slight, since the rarity of the anomalies (about one XYY in every 700 male births) precludes explanation in these terms of more than a tiny fraction of criminal cases. The contribution to this conference by Slater and Kahn, reporting a considerably raised incidence of minor trans-location abnormalities among remand home boys, changes the picture drastically. These kinds of chromosome deviations are comparatively common, and if they should prove to have a significant association with delinquency it would mean that chromosomal factors could have some relevance to quite large numbers of cases.

Owing to the complex and time-consuming techniques necessary for the identification of rare chromosomal variants, it will probably be a long time before examples from unselected populations are discovered in sufficient numbers to determine the true incidence and range of the mental and physical disorders associated with the possession of an extra Y chromosome. Meantime, close study and description of all known cases, even though they may have been found by searching among psychiatric and prison populations, can yield valuable clues. To that important task the participants in this Cropwood Conference have made a significant contribution.

D.J. West

NOTICE

For the readers' benefit, the contributors' references have been amalgamated into a single bibliography, but particular thanks are due to Dr. T.K. Maclachlan and Dr. A.W. Griffiths who assembled the majority of the items. The Editor wishes to thank Mr. Martin Wright, Librarian at the Institute of Criminology, and Miss Isobel Gawler for their help in compiling the bibliography.

CRIMINOLOGICAL IMPLICATIONS OF SEX CHROMOSOME
ABNORMALITIES: A REVIEW

T.K. Maclachlan

This paper is based on the work of the late Professor Court Brown and his staff in the Medical Research Council Clinical and Population Cytogenetics Unit. I have also relied heavily on the studies by Casey and co-workers in Sheffield and on the Scandinavians, Forssman, Hambert and Neilsen.

The history of human cytogenetics is short. The landmarks only need be reviewed. In 1949 Barr and Bertram discovered that there was a difference between the nuclei of male and female cells. The Barr body, a small darkly staining chromatin body, could be seen in a large percentage of female cells and not in cells from males. Barr introduced the technique of nuclear sexing by examination of cells from smears of the buccal mucosa. In 1956, Tjio and Levan showed that, contrary to earlier belief, humans had 46 chromosomes (i.e. 23 pairs). In 1959 the first descriptions of extra chromosomes in man were made. Lejeune and co-workers found trisomy chromosome 21 in mongolism. Jacobs and Strong discovered males with Klinefelter's syndrome to have an XXY complement. Ford and co-workers described an XO complement in a female with the features of Turner's syndrome and Jacobs and co-workers described the XXX female. In 1960 Moorhead and his colleagues described the technique of culturing white blood cells in order to obtain cell arrest in metaphase division. This produced the nucleus in a state suitable for counting and analysis of the chromosomes.

Thus in 1960 the stage was set for the origins of population cytogenetics. Since then large-scale surveys have been undertaken of various populations. The aim has been to seek individuals with abnormal chromosome constitution and to determine the relationship of various abnormalities with sub-groups of the population. By far the cheapest and simplest technique was the buccal-smear examination for Barr bodies, now called sex chromatin bodies. Subjects have been found with 1, 2, 3 and 4 chromatin bodies and it was soon realised that the number of bodies was always one less than the total number of X chromosomes in the cell. They thus represented the inactivated X chromosomes as postulated by Mary F. Lyon in 1962.

Since 1959 many populations have been surveyed by buccal-smear examination and abnormals discovered by this process have had further examination by lymphocyte culture. On a much more limited scale several centres have surveyed populations using the much more expensive and time-consuming analysis of chromosomes of lymphocytes. This technique, however, gives a complete picture of the chromosome constitution of the lymphocyte series of an individual.

The main problem in population studies has been to define the incidence of the various abnormalities in the general population. In view of the manifest difficulties of defining and obtaining the co-operation of a satisfactory sample of adults, most inferences as to the prevalence of any abnormality have been drawn from studies of the newborn. In studying adult, especially elderly adult, populations this method has some defects and I will mention two of them. First, many abnormal chromosome states may be associated with increased neonatal, infant or childhood deaths; for example, Turner's syndrome is known to be associated with severe morbidity owing to the associated cardiological abnormalities. It is not known if this effect is present in all subjects with extra chromosomes. Secondly, the mean maternal age is declining and certainly a proportion of many of the triploid states - trisomy 21, XXX, XXY etc. - are known to be associated with high maternal age. It is therefore valid to assume that the incidence of any abnormality in the newborn in 1968 may not relate closely to the incidence in an elderly population. Professor Court Brown drew attention to the need to guard against false conclusions (Court Brown & Smith, 1969), citing Ei Matsunaga in the Proceedings of the World Population Conference. Ei Matsunaga said that the 1948 Eugenic Protection Law of Japan had resulted in the proportion of live births to mothers aged over 35 years falling from 20% in 1947 to 6% in 1960. This change in maternal age had reduced the frequency of mongolism in the newborn by about half in his estimation. I feel that similar forces are at work in the United Kingdom.

As I have very little time and as I have doubts about the findings in population studies involving relatively small numbers I have confined myself to a discussion of the two most common sex-chromosome anomalies: 47,XXY as well as the most publicised anomaly 47,XYY. The chromatin positive male and female will be used at times in these surveys rather than pure XXY or XXX.

XYY

Studies of 47,XYY consisted initially of sporadic cases found fortuitously (Hauschka *et al.* 1962; Sandberg *et al.* 1961). Latterly in the last four years there have been surveys of groups, mainly of sociopathic offenders, the subnormal and the newborn. No syndrome emerged from the initial separate case histories. But in 1965 Dr. Court Brown and Dr. Patricia Jacobs were informed by Dr. M.D. Casey that he had found excess 48,XXYY's in a chromatin survey of the two Special Hospitals in England - Rampton and Moss Side (7 out of 21 chromatin positive males found in 942 patients).

Dr. Jacobs wondered if it was the double YY in these boys that made them "difficult to manage". In conjunction with the medical staff of the State Hospital at Carstairs (the Scottish Special Hospital) a survey of all male patients in that hospital was instituted. As is now well known, there were found 9 men of XYY constitution among 315 inmates; 7 of these were found among the 196 subnormal patients, the remaining 2 had "normal intelligence". (The total abnormals were 3 (47,XXY and 2 47,XYY's) among the 119 "normal I.Q." patients, while there were 9 (XY/XXY/XXXY, 48 XXYY and 7 47,XYY) among the 196 subnormals.)

It was found that the males with 47,XYY complement were on average 10.5 cm. taller than those patients with a 46,XY constitution. The male with the 48,XXYY complement was 194 cm. tall (6ft. 5½ins.). Dr. Casey and co-workers then examined 50 men from Moss Side and Rampton who were 183 cm. or more in height. He found 12 with 47,XYY constitution.

Now I feel that I must draw attention to the surveys which have concentrated on the selecting procedure of taking men above a certain height. While this no doubt increases the chances of a yield of XYY, it does make it very difficult to construe the findings. Thus one would expect 10% of the newborn to attain 183 cm. or more but we know that only 6.6% (21) of men at Carstairs were over this height. Similarly it is known that the mean height in hospitals for the sub-normal is much below the mean height of the general population. It might therefore be best in studying any population to select the top 10 percentile; we should then know where we stood in relating one population to another.

If this caveat is borne in mind, the results from the British Special Hospitals are remarkably similar to each other when considering the different sampling techniques and different legal categories involved. In the Carstairs sample, three further striking features were found in the 47,XYY males in comparison with their 46,XY companions (Price & Whatmore, 1967 *a* & *b*). The first was that the 47,XYYs were in trouble at an early age, 13 years as opposed to 18 years, secondly that most of their crimes were against property as opposed to crimes against persons. Thirdly, their families virtually did not have a criminal history. These latter two assertions have had some doubts cast upon them by subsequent reports. It would have been useful to have standardised for I.Q. and also to have considered other theoretical causes of delinquency, such as deprivation and parental handling. The tallness of 47,XYY males has stood up to further investigation.

In agreement with these findings of an association of one group of behaviour disorders - a very selected group - with a high incidence of XYY males are the following studies of males in other criminal institutions: Grendon Underwood (Bartlett *et al*. 1968), Wandsworth Prison (Griffiths & Zaremba 1967), Pentridge Prison, Melbourne (Weiner *et al*. 1968), Approved Schools (Hunter 1968), Ohio State Penitentiary (Goodman *et al*. 1967), Oregon State Hospital (Thompson 1967, quoted Court Brown 1968b). In addition there are the individual cases that were selected for study on account of their behaviour: Richards & Stewart (1966), Forsman (1967), Person (1967), Cowie & Kahn (1968), Leff & Scott (1968).

In marked contrast to these studies are the recent surveys carried out by Dr. Patricia Jacobs in the Scottish prisons, borstals, young offenders' institutions and allocation centres (Court Brown & Smith 1969). In Dr. Jacobs' study only 5 47,XYY males were found among 1759 studies; 510 of these men had been selected for height, so the incidence in the total population was probably nearer 1/1000 and thus not significantly different from the studies of the newborn. As far as I know this is the only unselected delinquent population study that has been reported. Though Dr. Court Brown reported a number of refusers among these groups, they had a random height distribution and he did not think that their numbers altered the significance of the findings.

We now wait for further surveys of the total prison population in a defined area before the significance of these recent findings can be properly evaluated. However, as Professor Court Brown (Court Brown & Smith, 1969) has said, it may be that the criminal population is very different from that in the Special Hospitals. Thus only two of the nine 47,XYY males found in Carstairs Special Hospital had ever been to prison. Six of the men had been in hospitals for the subnormal and four had been transferred directly from such a hospital to the State Hospital. The reason for their transfer was that their behaviour posed difficulties for their management in the hospital for subnormal. Three other men had been sent directly to the Special Hospital for assault (2 for sexual assault). It is also worth saying that, of the original nine men found in 1965, only four still resided in Carstairs in 1968. The others had all been transferred. It seems then that in Scotland the 47,XYY's had been found predominantly among "hard to manage" males. In line with this is the finding that 47,XYY males are found more commonly in subnormal hospitals that have closed-door policies (Close *et al*., 1967).

It also seems significant to me that 7 of the Carstairs 47,XYY males came from the subnormal I.Q. wing (204 subjects) while only 2 47,XYY males came from the "normal" I.Q. wing (111 subjects). Similarly in Casey's work 12 out of 50 males 6ft. tall and over were found at the predominantly subnormal hospitals of Rampton and Moss Side, while only 4 out of 50 patients 6ft. tall and over were found to be 47,XYY at the predominantly "normal I.Q." Special Hospital, Broadmoor. Though the differences are not statistically significant they may (to use a dangerous phrase) show a trend.

There have been very few case histories of XYY males described. Most of these have been inmates of institutions. Thus J. Nielsen (1969) described some of the main characteristics of his 2 cases. The first was a 26-year-old unmarried mechanic 47,XYY. His father was a labourer who was said to have provided a secure home along with the mother; he was no. 2 of four siblings. He was said to have developed normally apart frcm enuresis until the age of 16, and to have had his first sex experience at 15. From the age of 20 he started drinking to overcome shyness and inferiority feelings. At the ages of 24 and 26 he made suicide attempts while working on ships in South America. He was admitted to a mental hospital aged 26 and has shown an immature dependence on the hospital ever since. He produces symptoms which obtain his re-admission soon after discharge. His delinquency symptoms consisted in stealing and picking pockets when under the influence of alcohol and when suffering from symptoms of anxiety. He specifically mentioned the tranquillising effect of the delinquent act on his anxiety symptoms. His I.Q. was 93 Full Scale W.A.I.S.

Dr. Neilsen's second case was the son of a carpenter and was aged 26. He was found to have a 47,XYY constitution when in a mental hospital. He was no. 2 of eight siblings and his immediate family was said to be healthy and intact, but some more distant relatives suffered from mental illness, epilepsy and mental retardation. The patient as a boy had a disharmonious relationship with his father and suffered at school through being "word blind". He still suffers from this disorder. He was teased by other children as he was poor at gymnastic activities as well as reading. He had feelings of inferiority and gave up easily in adversity. From the age of twelve he had many admissions to neurological wards for symptoms similar to narcolepsy. No abnormal neurological signs were found at any time and the E.E.G. was always normal. I.Q. measured at different times was given as 92, 84 and 94. From the age of 18 he started drinking as he felt better accepted by people when under the influence of alcohol. He had his first sexual relationship at the age of 23 and married the girl as she became pregnant. He became more dependent upon alcohol following the birth of his daughter. His wife left him and following this he threatened to commit suicide while drunk and was admitted to hospital. After he left hospital he "fell in love" with a 14-year-old girl. They were discovered having sexual intercourse and he was taken to court. He was given a suspended sentence on condition that he was under psychiatric care. Four months later after discharge from the forensic unit, he re-appeared at the hospital in tears - in despair. He was dependent on the hospital and made histrionic attempts at suicide thereafter to gain re-admission.

XXY

Jacobs and Strong (1959) made the first chromosome analysis of a patient with Klinefelter's syndrome: they found that he had 47 chromosomes and the sex chromosome constitution was XXY. This was soon confirmed by the authors (unpublished) and by Ford *et al*. 1959, Harnden *et al*. 1960. Several hundred individuals have been reported with a 47,XXY constitution since.

Chromatin positive males are found on average in 1.9/1000 babies. Of these the majority are 47,XXY (1.3/1000) and the next most common aneuploid male is the mosaic 46,XY/47,XXY. All other variations such as the XXYY, XXXY, XXXXY are very uncommon as are the mosaics with this constitution. Of particular interest are the chromatin positive males with the constitution XX and there are about 20 such people reported in the literature. None of these variants will be discussed here in view of their rarity and in view of the difficulty in coming to conclusions concerning the more common sex chromosome anomalies, the 47,XXY and the 47,XYY males.

Not all males with Klinefelter's syndrome have the 47,XXY constitution but I will include references to criminality in Klinefelters in my review of the association between 47,XXY and putative criminality.

In 1953 Zublin described 6 cases of Klinefelter's syndrome with 2 guilty of larceny; since then the following have also mentioned antisocial acts in conjunction with either Klinefelter's syndrome or the 47,XXY male: Illchmann-Christ (1959), Rasch (1959), Mosier *et al.* (1960), Court Brown (1962), Rohde (1963), Wegmann & Smith (1963), De La Chapelle (1963).

It might be profitable to divide the antisocial behaviour into two groups from now on - delinquent acts and sexually deviant behaviour.

Delinquent Acts

Dr. Court Brown (1962) reported that in a study of 47,XXY males in subnormal and mental institutions 30% had committed antisocial acts such as larceny, arson and indecent exposure. Forsman (1963) found an incidence of 15/1000 XXYs in institutions for "hard to manage" males of subnormal intelligence. Pritchard (1962) and Neilsen (1964) confirmed the high incidence of character disorder and alcoholism in the 47,XXY males in mental hospitals.

Casey (1966b) reported 21 chromatin positive males among the 942 inmates of the two Special Hospitals, Rampton and Moss Side; but the nature of their antisocial activities did not differ significantly from their chromatin-negative fellow inmates. They did, however, seem to abscond more often than their fellows. Bartlett found two 47,XXY males and one 46,XY/47,XXY mosaic among 204 inmates of Grendon Underwood Prison for psychiatric treatment (Bartlett *et al.*, 1968).

Recently Hunter (1966) has examined the antisocial acts of 17 chromatin positive males admitted to subnormal institutions. Seven had had court appearances, 6 for larceny, 1 for aggression; 12 out of the 17 had shown antisocial behaviour.

Close also reported an increased incidence of detention under court order among the chromatin positive males in two subnormal hospitals when comparing chromatin negative controls. This was significant only among patients with an I.Q. above 50 (Close *et al.*, 1968).

Neilsen (1969) reports that 11 out of 17 47,XXY males found in a prevalence study of a mental hospital had been sentenced for different types of criminality. Among all his 28 cases of 47,XXY males, 15 (54%) had been sentenced for "criminality". The criminality was not serious. The question of the relationship of criminal behaviour is best discussed after looking at Tables I, II and III. The information on these tables is based mainly on that supplied by Dr. Court Brown in 1967.

14

TABLE I

XXY and the Chromatin Positive Males: Singly chromatin-positive males in world surveys quoted in Court Brown (1967*b*)

Total studied		No.	per 1000	
Newborn	41,688	71	1.7	Various authors
Hospital admission	4,137	7	1.7	Baikie *et al.* (1966)
Military conscripts	2,752	6	2.2	Hambert (1965)
U.S. army recruits	1,000	2	2.0	Kaplan & Norfleet
15 surveys of hospitals for subnormals	13,349	101	7.6	Various authors
4 surveys of subnormal I.Q. 50+	1,822	32	17.6	Various authors
Hard to manage subnormal 50+ Swedes	958	16	16.6	Forssman & Hambert (1967)
Moss Side, Rampton and 183 low I.Q. Carstairs	1,126	23	20.4	Casey, Segal, Street & Blank (1966*b*)

The most significant point is that though there is a marked difference in the incidence of 47,XXY males in groups of delinquents compared with all other groups - including total subnormality populations - there is no difference between the incidence in delinquent populations and subnormal populations of I.Q. 50+. Therefore one may postulate that the delinquency in 47,XXY males may be a function of their low I.Q. Equally one might postulate that the reason for the presence of high grade I.Q. XXY males in subnormality hospitals is related to behaviour difficulties.

TABLE II

The Frequency of Chromatin-Positive Patients related to their I.Q. among male patients in hospitals for the mentally subnormal.[†]

I.Q.	Total Males	No.[*]	No. per 1000
< 20	901	2	2.2
20-49	1,767	16	9.0
50 or more	864	13	15.2
All ranges	3,532	31	8.8

[†] Barr *et al.* (1959, 1960 and 1962), Mosier *et al.* (1960a), Breg *et al.* (1963).
[*] 23 singly chromatin-positive, 7 doubly positive and 1 trebly positive.

In Sweden where the policy is to maintain the subnormal I.Q. population in the community unless they are too hard to manage, it is interesting that Forssman and Hambert should find an incidence of those in institutions that is similar to the incidence in our own Special Security Hospitals.

TABLE III

Nuclear sexing surveys in Swedish hospitals for mentally subnormal hard-to-manage males.

Hospital	Total males	No.* Chromatin-Positive	No. Abnormal per 1000
I.Q. ⩾ 50			
Salberga	381	7	18.4
Vastra Ny.	182	4	22.0
Kallshagen	304	6	19.7
Salbohed	52	1	19.2
Vingaker	39	1	25.6
All	958	19	19.8
I.Q. < 50			
Vipeholm	620	3	4.8

* I.Q. 50 or more: 16 singly chromatin-positive and 3 doubly positive.
I.Q. < 50: 2 singly positive and 1 doubly positive.

From Neilsen (1969) and others it seems that 47,XXY male in institutions may be characterised by immature behaviour with histrionic and feckless traits; but others have found no difference between chromatin-positive subjects and controls. It seems at this time that one cannot dissociate "behaviour disorders" from subnormal intelligence.

TABLE IV

Surveys of various criminal groups - Chromatin-positive

	Group	Total males	No. singly Chromatin +ve
De La Chapelle (1963)	"Criminals"	383	1
Wegmann & Smith (1963)	Juvenile delinquents, Wisconsin	505	0
	Young adult male, Wisconsin State Reformatory	813	2
Jacobs, quoted in Court Brown (1969)	New entrants Scottish borstals	607	3
Court Brown	Approved schools	340	2
Court Brown (1968b)	Scottish prison allocation centre	302	0
Court Brown	Scottish prisoners 178 cm. or more	419	2
Court Brown	Scottish young offenders' institutions	91	0
Hunter (1968)	Approved schools	1,021	2
Total Males	4,481		
Total Chromatin +ve	12		
Frequency	2.7/1000		

Sexual Delinquent Acts

Sexual disorders have been commonly reported: Illchmann-Christ (1959) reported on 2 paedophilic; Rasch (1959) reported exhibitionism to children; Mosier *et al.* (1960) reported a high incidence (6 out of 600) of chromatin-positive males among sexual offenders; Stumpfl (1960) 1 homosexual; Dowling & Knox (1963) 1 transvestite and homosexual; Money (1963) 4 homosexuals and 1 transvestite; Money & Pollit (1964); Gilbert-Dreyfus *et al.* (1965); Hambert (1966).

Neilsen (1964 & 1969), Roth (1964) and Hunter (1968) have also reported an increased incidence of deviant sexual behaviour among chromatin-positive males. Jacobs, reporting further on the patients in Carstairs Special Hospital, among other details gave the penal and institutional records of the 3 chromatin-positive males. Two had been convicted of sexual assaults, one of whom had also absconded regularly and had thrown a 14-year-old boy into a river. The other was first convicted of sexual offences at the age of 33; he also had been charged with fire-raising and theft (Jacobs *et al.*, 1968).

Recently Melnyk and co-workers reported again on a survey of Atascadero State Hospital, California, where Mosier had first reported on a chromatin-positive survey (Melnyk *et al.*, 1969). This time all males over 6ft. tall (200) had been surveyed for chromosome constitution; 2 47,XXYs had been found; both had been guilty of male paedophilia and one had interfered with his sister. The findings from California (Mosier *et al.*, 1960b), however, infer one very important point. They found that only one of their cases was borderline subnormal I.Q. - the rest had normal I.Q. This suggests that for sexual offences an I.Q. factor can be discounted.

Neilsen's survey of a mental hospital produced 11 delinquent XXY males. He reported that the criminality was not severe; but three patients out of his total reported were paedophilics. Significantly, maybe, none of these men was sufficiently potent to have normal sexual relationships with adult women. Neilsen (1969) queries whether worry about lack of masculinity as well as their immaturity and sensitivity may lead to an increased risk of 'criminality'. He compared the incidence of sexual crime among the XXY males (27%) with the incidence in the general population (7%). The sample discussed is small and one therefore should put little credence in conclusions drawn from it, especially in view of some studies that do not substantiate this line of thought (Casey, 1966).

Summary

XXY and chromatin-positive males

Many have cited a relationship between chromatin-positive male subjects and delinquency. The relationship is now in some doubt since Professor Court Brown pointed out the variation in the incidence of chromatin-positive subjects with different I.Q. groups. Most delinquency centres that have been studied have been mainly composed of high-grade defectives. The incidence in most delinquent societies does not differ significantly from the incidence in the above 50 I.Q. population of subnormal hospitals. One therefore postulates that their presence in delinquency centres may be a function of their I.Q. In line with this is the finding of Wegmann and Smith of only 2 chromatin-positive males among 1318 delinquents, mostly of normal or superior I.Q. Further studies are therefore indicated; but the inference may be that behaviour disturbance is the reason for many high-grade defectives being in an institution. This is borne out to some degree as the patients under a compulsory order cluster in the high ability range of a subnormal hospital (Close *et al.*, 1968, Darenth Park).

Sex offences

Mosier has shown in California that there is an excess of chromatin-positive males among sex offenders in subnormal and normal I.Q. institutions. Some other smaller studies do not substantiate this. The question remains open.

XXX and chromatin-positive females

As was the case with chromatin-positive males, there seems to be the same argument *vis-à-vis* high-grade subnormality and the XXXs. The number of female delinquents studied has been very small and there is not enough evidence to draw any concrete conclusions.

XYY

The leading article in the *British Medical Journal* of February 1969 summarised the legal position - behaviour rather than chromosome constitution is important in law. The number of these subjects that have been found is still very small but there are several points about those 47,XYYs found in Special Hospitals that I should like to emphasise. Firstly in Carstairs:

7 47,XYY were found in the subnormal wing out of 196 studied.
2 47,XYY were found in the disturbed wing out of 119 studied.

These men tended to be tall and this has been borne out by subsequent reports.

12 47,XYY males were found among 50 6ft. and over subnormal men in Moss Side and Rampton.
4 47,XYY males were found among 50 6ft. and over disturbed men in Broadmoor.

Price and Whatmore (1967a) reported the striking finding that the siblings of XYY males have had very few convictions, while control inmates of Carstairs had siblings with multiple convictions. They therefore concluded that the family background was not likely to be the cause of delinquency in the XYY. This finding has not been confirmed by the studies in Rampton and Moss Side.

Unhappily it was not possible to examine the families of the control population in Carstairs and only some details were known of the XYYs (Jacobs *et al*. 1968, Appendix II). There does seem some query about the backgrounds that included parental death and illegitimacy. More needs to be known about the families of XYY and control subjects from the same population group in which they were found.

However, the high yield of 9 XYY subjects out of 315 males in Carstairs contrasts sharply with the apparent incidence among the newborn at this time. In Edinburgh, 3 XYY have been found among 2400 newborn male babies. It is significant that two of these were found among the last 500 studied, as this emphasises the point that one needs large numbers in order to establish the true incidence. It seems from various unofficial communications of other centres that the incidence in the newborn may lie between 1 and 1.5 per 1000, compared with the incidence in Carstairs of 28 per 1000, at least 20 times as large.

Among other Scottish penal groups the yield is not nearly so impressive: i.e. 607 new entrants to Borstals, 1 XYY. This is not significantly different from newborn. It is worth noting that the four cases of YY (i.e. 3 XYY and 1 XXYY) described in the *Lancet* in the last twelve months had not been to court or to a maladjusted institution.

My personal belief coincides with that of Dr. P.D. Scott, mentioned in the Cropwood Conference of Psychopathic Offenders, 1968. At the moment it seems feasible to put an extra Y chromosome among the many factors that may lead to behaviour abnormalities. The extra chromosome may lead to a high-grade subnormal who stands out from his peers on account of his tallness and cannot deal with any further difficulties. From the reports of murders and impulsive behaviour generally these may be found to have a low ability to deal with frustration or other emotional crises.

Finally the question to be answered is: If the incidence of XYYs in the population is 1.5/1000 and only about 70 XYYs have been found in the United Kingdom - one expects 1,500 among every 1,000,000 males - where are these other XYYs?

APPENDIX I

XXY

Hambert, G. (1966)

No.	Age	Psychosis	Behaviour	Emotion	Sex	Delinquency	E.E.G.	Source	Other Illness
1	50	paranoid psychosis	hypochondriacal	nervous	hypo	alcoholism	-	mental h.	
2	55	paranoid psychosis megalomania		jealous suspicious	"	-	-	"	
3	54	manic psychosis	nil abnormal	slightly affected	"	-	-	"	
4	55	paranoid + dementia	-	jealous	"	-	-	"	
5	74	paranoid psychosis going demented	-	good natured but aggressive at times	"	not known	not known	"	
6	64	drug addiction	-	obedient + compliant	XXY	-	-	"	
7	35	neurotic	shy and unsure	shy	hypo	threatened murder	-	"	
8	49	paranoid + megalomania	not noted	not noted	"	-	border line	"	
9	57	"	-	-	"	sexual assault	abnormal	"	
10	41	schizophrenia	not difficult	passive & good natured	"	-	"	"	
11	29	-	drunken + sexual cravings	quiet & shy	normal	drunk + sexual assault	"	"	

No.	Age	Psychosis	Behaviour	Emotion	Sex	Delinquency	E.E.G.	Source	Other Illness
12	31	paranoid	avoids people	easily embarrassed good natured	very low	sexual to women	not reported	mental h.	hypo-thyroidism obesity
13	52	psychotic	attacks of rage	stubborn, child-ish, hot temper	-	-	-	"	
XY/XXY 14	68	dementia	passive	pleasant, quiet		-	-	"	mental defect
15	58	paranoid schizophrenia	good	good tempered attacks of rage; said to be father of a daughter		-	abnormal	"	cerebral haemorrhage gastritis
16	67	paranoid & affected illness	-	shy & retiring flares up at times	almost nil	-	"	"	
17	56	paranoid psychosis	childish	usually calm & orderly: at times aggressive & quarrelsome	-	-	"	"	
18	23		-	calm, quiet, passive	hypo	robbery	"	"	epilepsy
19	78	paranoid psychosis	excessive drinking	good father & husband	"	threatened to murder	"	"	diabetes of old age
20	54	manic depressive	well behaved, shy	friendly, reticent	"	-	"	"	
21	76	dementia	occasional agg-ression & destructiveness	bearable	"	stealing	"	"	-
22	36	-	out-going indiv-idual, loses temper easily		"	-	"	"	head injury
23	72	dementia	-	hot temper		-	"	"	diabetes of old age

No.	Age	Psychosis	Behaviour	Emotion	Sex	Delinquency	E.E.G.	Source	Other Illness
24	23	-	friendly, low I.Q.	calm, easy to manage	hypo	stealing	normal	maladjusted retarded	-
25	27	mild paranoia	liar	sensitive & childish	normal	attempted rape, rape & murder	abnormal	"	-
26	41	-	irritable negativistic	outbursts of rage	very low	-	"	"	-
27	21	suspicious	can be aggressive	labile	hypo	stealing, threatened rape & knifing	"	"	-
28	24	-	lacking initiative, adjusted to hospital	can be aggressive	"	aggressive sexual advances & assaults on women	"	"	-
29	33	-	friendly & compliable	stubborn & sometimes aggressive	"	indecent assault, exposure	normal	"	duodenal ulcer
XXXY 30	46	psychotic	hard to manage can be destructive	easily irritated	"	-	abnormal	"	tremor
31	32	-	could easily turn aggressive	labile	homo	petty thefts & homosexual	"	"	-
XXXY 32	19	-	easily became aggressive: hard to manage: occasionally threatening	explosive temper	hypo	-	not recorded	"	-
33	22	? psychotic	usually easy to handle	infantile occasionally aggressive	"	stealing paedophilia	border-line	"	-
34	20	-	solitary	unhappy, sulky	"	stealing	"	"	-
35	20	-	unfriendly & antisocial	unhappy, sulky uncommunicative	normal	stealing	"	"	-

No.	Age	Psychosis	Behaviour	Emotion	Sex	Delinquency	E.E.G.	Source	Other Illness
36	21	-	aggressive, destructive & violent	variable, nervous & excitable	nil	aggression, violence, indecent behaviour	abnormal	maladjusted retarded	stammer backward XXYY
37	31	-	alcoholic, aggression at times	cringing & passive towards people in superior positions	-	number of crimes while intoxicated	"	"	alcoholic retarded
38	44	-	well behaved	calm but depressed, social	normal	petty crimes & fraud	normal	"	stammer
39	25	-	can be irritable & violent	usually calm	little known	various crimes, indecent assault on boy of 8	-	"	-
40	60	manic depressive with paranoia	normal	friendly	normal	none	normal	"	none
41	17	-	few outbursts of temper: aggression	little emotional control	normal but homosexual tendencies	-	abnormal	"	speech defect until he was 7
42	44	intermittent porphyria with depression	-	impulsive but otherwise good emotional contact	hypo	none	normal	mental h.	porphyria eczema & asthma
43	38	-	attacks of rage	tense, worried & unhappy, easily impressed	normal	alcoholism	abnormal	"	stomach ulcer
44	48	schizo-affective	apathetic, passive, unenterprising	passive	nil	-	normal	"	had had epileptic fits

No.	Age	Psychosis	Behaviour	Emotion	Sex	Delinquency	E.E.G.	Source	Other Illness
45	67	paranoid schizophrenic	occasional megalomania & threatening	dull & apathetic	not known	-	normal	mental h.	none
46	54	depressive	co-operative	friendly	normal	-	borderline	"	asthma
47	47	mild depression	nervous, drinking	timid, quiet	"	-	abnormal	"	tremor unassociated with his alcoholism
48	32	-	co-operative	pleasant & cheerful	nil	-	severely abnormal	epileptic inst.	severe epilepsy spastic tetraplegia: atrophy of the brain
49	20	-	usually calm, can be defiant & troublesome	friendly	N.K.	stealing	abnormal	"	epilepsy
50	42	-	demented	not known	not known	stealing	presumed abnormal	"	G.M. epilepsy dementia
51	42	-	dull & lethargic easily influenced	good nature	"	-	abnormal	"	-
52	9	-		-	-	-	-	-	-
53	22	-	lacking initiative, exhibitionist	immature little contact	hypo	stealing exposure	abnormal	miscellaneous	hypothyroidism Scheuermann's disease
54	19	-	unstable	immature, superficial contact	normal	stealing	"	"	-
55	53	-	periods of calm & aggression	violent temper	unknown	not known	"	hard to manage retarded	-

No.	Age	Psychosis	Behaviour	Emotion	Sex	Delinquency	E.E.G.	Source	Other Illness
56	11	no psychosis	restless,aggressive, destructive	labile	not known	not known	abnormal	hard to manage retarded	not known
57	53	"	sensible	normal	normal	nil	abnormal	miscellaneous	-
58	20	"	normal	shy & not demanding	"	"	"	"	heart disease
59	19	"	"	temper	not known	"	"	"	none
60	18	"	energetic, hard working	cheerful, friendly	normal	"	"	controls	none
61	18	"	slightly weak & retiring	shy but easy to get in contact with	"	"	"	"	dorsal kyphosis
62	18	"	felt a weakling	shy but easy to get in contact with	"	"	"	"	-
63	18	"	tired easily	shy but easily angered	"	-	"	"	XY/XXY mosaic
64	18	"	passive, unenterprising	passive, occasional anger	hypo	-	not recorded	"	-
65	18	not known	not known	not known	not known	not known		"	father refused interview
66	37	-	occasionally very aggressive & threatening	immature	hypo	stealing	not known	miscellaneous	alcoholic
67	51	mildly paranoid	feminine interests	brooding & became very aggressive	"	nil	normal	"	malformation of the left leg

No.	Age	Psychosis	Behaviour	Emotion	Sex	Delinquency	E.E.G.	Source	Other Illness
68	53	nil but attempted suicide	helpless: unable to take care of himself	very sensitive	not known	nil	abnormal	miscellaneous	nil
69	16	none	aggressive	irritable	"	not known	not known	maladjusted retarded	maladjusted mother paranoid
70	42	paranoid	suspicious	discontented, irritable	hypo	exhibition	not recorded	miscellaneous	nil
71	27	no psychosis	not known	not known	not known	not known	normal	"	not known
72	35	no psychosis	not known	not known	not known	not known	abnormal	"	operated on for arterio-venous aneurism (cerebral)
73	17	"	very retarded	"	"	"	"	hard to manage retarded	not known
74	65	paranoid psychosis megalomania	self-absorbed	irritable	"	"	not known	mental h.	none
75	59	schizophrenic	retiring, solitary	passive, indifferent	"	"	normal	miscellaneous	"

Zuppinger, K. *et al.* (1967)

No.	Age	Psychosis	Behaviour	Emotion	Sex	Delinquency	E.E.G.	Source	Other Illness
1	17	nil	immature, easily tired	shy, quiet	hypo	nil	border line normal; XS diffuse slow frequencies for his age	endocrine clinic	nil gigantism
2	27	"	unemployed: dismissed from high school for bad conduct	felt sexually inadequate	?normal	school: bad conduct	moderately abnormal paroxysmal activity with stroboscope	"	nil herniorrhaphy aet. 10
3	29	no psychosis	childlike & trusting	friendly	normal	nil	probably normal (mild swelling on hyperventilation)	"	nil rheumatic fever obesity somnolence
4	30	"	feminine behaviour, female impersonation	gentle, confiding, wished to be female	transvestite ?homosexual	reform school	not obtained	"	nil transvestitism
5	39	repeated depressions with suicide attempts: alcoholic & drug dependence	alcoholic, ineffectual	ran away from hospital: cannot face life	said to be normal	reform schools stealing	moderately abnormal (much generalised 6/7 secs. slow activity)	"	since age 10 jerky movements of arms. alcoholism
6	36	no psychosis	normal	poised, friendly	hypo	nil	moderately abnormal (3/5 secs. slowing on hyperventilation)	"	hernia varicose veins bilateral patella dislocation
7	34	"	satisfactory	friendly but timid: hypochondriasis	"	"	normal	"	nil pilo nidal cyst G.O. hypertrophic gastritis

No.	Age	Psychosis	Behaviour	Emotion	Sex	Delinquency	E.E.G.	Source	Other Illness
8	35	no psychosis	steadily employed, divorced	normal	normal	nil	mildly abnormal diffuse slow activity	endocrine clinic	nil severe acne
9	52	"	histrionic attention-seeking	ambitious & successful	"	"	mildly abnormal diffuse slow activity with spiky bursts	"	renal colic obesity hyperoxaluria
10	42	"	marriage annulled (impotence)	ran away from home & school	hypo	"	normal	"	obesity blackout
11	37	"	hyperandriacal	complaining	"	"	"	"	D.U. renal colic
12	43	"	divorced 1st marriage: racing car driver	normal	normal	"	"	"	nil strabismus haemorrhoids l. arm tremor heart-burn
13	36	"	divorced, heavy drinking	nil	nil	"	moderately abnormal; excess high voltage: slow activity especially L temporo-occipital	"	mild diabetes & bilateral tremor phlebitis stasis ulcers C.V.A. hemiplegia
14	52	attacks of depression	manner aggressive, blustering: married	friendly	?normal	helped to avoid prosecution for incorrect tax return	not obtained		epilepsy hyperoxaluria hypothyroidism narcolepsy
15	50	schizophrenia & chronic alcoholism	divorced, had been heavy drinker: welfare supported	sad & anxious	hypo	"welfare supported"	normal	"	diabetic GTT goitre

No.	Age	Psychosis	Behaviour	Emotion	Sex	Delinquency	E.E.G.	Source	Other Illness
16	50	no psychosis	ineffectual, childish chatter	dependent, immature	very low	nil	moderately abnormal; slow alpha activity	endocrine clinic	varicose veins obesity 450 pounds cholecystectomy stasis ulcers
17	53	"	very talkative unemployed, welfare dependent: divorced		nil	"	normal	"	diabetes obesity G.U. renal colic
18	50	nil	Been looking for work for 23 years: constant flow of rapid irrelevant talk	friendly & childlike	hypo	"	"	"	varicose veins & ulcers, dermatitis obesity, tremor cataract
19	56	no psychosis	divorced, over-talkative	unknown	"	"	mildly abnormal; sharp waves of stroboscopic stimulation	"	varicose veins mild diabetes cataract
20	56	"	divorced, many jobs, frequent alcoholic, talked incessantly	gentle & excessively polite	"	jailed for stealing & wrecking his wife's car	normal	"	E.A. tremor obesity varicose veins stripping
21	59	"	irregular work, left his wife: "she was a sex fiend"	friendly & frank: preoccupation with his gonadal problem	"	reform school for truancy	"	"	chronic brain syndrome varicose veins diabetic collilithiasis asthma, emphysema bronchiectasis died of haemoptysis
22	60	"	employed married	hypo	"	none	not reported	"	pneumonia, haemoptysis bronchiectasis alcoholism

No.	Age	Psychosis	Behaviour	Emotion	Sex	Delinquency	E.E.G.	Source	Other Illness
23	70	no psychosis	not divorced after 40 years of marriage	not known	severely hypo	nil	moderately abnormal episodes of slow waves	endocrine clinic	pancreatitis gastritis D.U. aortic stenosis hepato-spleno-megaly osteoporosis
24	73	"	frail, rejected for army in the 1st world war: married at 28, said to have had a daughter	not known	not known	not known	not known	"	none D.U., chronic under-nourishment

APPENDIX II

Recent Notes

I   Court Brown (1968b) drew attention to subjects with XYY or XYY mosaic constitution who have a female phenotype. He came to the conclusion that in mosaics the variation in phenotype "may be a function of the relative proportions of the two cell lines in the developing gonads during embryogenesis". Then it can be postulated that in the female phenotype 45 XY cells are predominant in the gonads during embryogenesis and that 47 XYY cells were predominant in the male phenotype.

He does believe, however, that there is evidence (Vignetti *et al.*, 1964; Forsberg *et al.*, 1964 and Franks *et al.* 1967) that there are subjects with the female phenotype characterised by an XYY sex chromosome complement in gonadal tissues.

II Court Brown (*ibid.*): "It is fair to suggest - that our knowledge of the range of phenotypes associated with the XYY complement is possibly far from complete and that in concentrating on males with gross antisocial conduct, as currently is being done, we may be guilty of biased selection."

III Court Brown *et al.* (1968c): "There is no evidence which indicates that the XYY male is bound inexorably to develop antisocial traits and in fact our own experience in Edinburgh suggests a spectrum of behaviour ranging from the apparently normal through those with a mild personality disorder to those who are severe psychopaths."

IV British Medical Journal [Legal Correspondent] (1968): "Studies showing the incidence of chromosome abnormalities among offenders *may provide supporting* evidence of the likelihood of mental subnormality in the case of an individual who has a chromosome abnormality."

V Wiener *et al.* (1969): "It is certain that genetic research has done little more than get started and it is also very likely that in the months and years to come further abnormalities will be recognised - abnormalities affecting behaviour and possibly correlating with anti-sociality, perhaps aggressive and criminal anti-sociality.

One may simply summarise the position by saying that we are far too ignorant at this time to say with any meaningful certainty - "This man is 'normal' or even 'responsible'."

VI Scott & Kahn: "Thus it is probable that the XYY complement may have a less important medico-legal implication than at first might have been supposed....It may rather take its place amongst the multitude of predisposing, partial or contributory factors, such as lesser degrees of impaired intelligence, a long history of behaviour disorders resistant to remedial measures."

Backgrounds of Criminal XYYs

P.A. Jacobs *et al.* Carstairs Special Hospital

1 120/65   Age 31   Father, builder's labourer.
Mother and father alive and well.
Second in sibship of 5.

12 convictions including 4 theft and 4 sexual assault

2 122/65		Father, foundry worker. Died when patient 14. Mother died when patient 6. Second in sibship of 9.

Theft. Mental depression.
Backward at school.
No temper control even over trifles.
Truant.

14 convictions - theft and housebreaking.

3 123/65   Father, fitter in merchant navy.
Parents separated when patient over 7.
Father drinks ++ Alcoholic.
Eldest in sibship of 5.

Backward at school - difficult to manage.

9 convictions. All for theft. First at age 8.
Borstal, Subnormal Hospital, State Hospital.

4 132/65   Age 20   Father, ship's carpenter.
Mother died when patient 16.
Eldest of two sibs.

School record good - top of class in 'B' stream.

5 convictions. First aged 14. 1 assault.

5 134/65   Age 34   Father, welder; aged 40 when propositus born.
Fifth in sibship of 5.

Evacuated aged 6 - so distressed, returned after
4/12.

Slow at school. Truant.

1 charge - Lewd practices - homosexual.

6 141/65   Age 31   Father, Lt. Col. Army, retired. Rose from ranks.
Position very important.
Father had high expectations of his children
especially the eldest.
Mother died when patient aged 20.
No. 1 in sibship of 5.

AN INVESTIGATION OF A GROUP OF XYY PRISONERS

* A.W. Griffiths, H.M. Prison, Wandsworth, London.

B.W. Richards, St. Lawrence's Hospital, Caterham, Surrey.

† J. Zaremba,   "   "   "   "   "

† T. Abramowicz, "   "   "   "   "

A. Stewart   "   "   "   "   "

A chromosomal survey of 355 tall male inmates of a large London prison disclosed 9 individuals of XYY karyotype. When these were compared with a control group, significant differences emerged in respect of intelligence levels, previous psychiatric illness, achievement relative to other members of the family, and the number of previous convictions. Certain other differences of interest but of lesser magnitude are also described.

Previous studies

Cytogenetic surveys, summarised on the next page and analysed in Table 1, suggest that males of XYY chromosome constitution tend to be concentrated amongst tall detained delinquents especially those with psychiatric disorder.

The present investigation

A survey of tall prisoners has been carried out at a large London prison whose population although heterogeneous is largely composed of recidivists from London and the Home Counties. Certain disruptions of the available facilities necessitated the division of the surveyed population into the following sub-groups.

I. Consenting prisoners of height 6' and over, admitted in 1967 during certain limited periods governed by the availability of laboratory and other services.

II. Consenting randomly selected prisoners of height 5' 11" and over who were resident in March 1968.

III. Consenting prisoners of height 5' 11" and over, admitted from 15th September 1968 to the 18th October 1969 who were available.

Leucocytes were cultured from venous blood ml.10 by the method of Moorhead *et al.*, preparations being air-dried and stained by Giemsa. Results are given in Table II.

Each subject of XYY constitution was matched from the same sub-group with a control of normal karyotype whose age lay within 12 months and height within 3". These criteria being satisfied, the chosen control was he who was admitted to the prison as closely as possible to the subject. Ages ranged from 23 to 46 years with a mean of 30. The mean height of subjects was 73.4 in. and controls 72.3 in.; 6 out of 9 subjects were taller than their controls.

Data, which as far as possible were expressed in quantitative terms, were obtained from each individual by means of a standard questionnaire devised for the present study. Details were supplemented where possible from other media which included police records, probation reports, parole

* The author has been in receipt of a grant from the Home Office Research Unit.

† The author has been in receipt of a grant from the Mental Health Research Fund.

Summary of previous studies*

(suggesting a relatively high incidence of the XYY anomaly amongst detained delinquents)

Source	Population	XYY subjects	Special features
Jacobs, Brunton, Melville, Brittain & McClemont (1965) Price & Whatmore (1967) Price (1968)	315 mentally ill or subnormal patients of a maximum security hospital for those with dangerous, violent or criminal propensities.	9	Tall. Almost no criminal convictions in relatives. Early age at first conviction. Few crimes of personal violence. Persistent criminal behaviour. E.C.G. changes.
Casey, Blank, Street, Segall, McDougall, McGrath & Skinner (1966)	Height 50 mentally subnormal patients det-6' or ained for anti-social behaviour. over 50 mentally ill patients detained for anti-social behaviour.	12 4	
	24 prisoners	2	
Court Brown (1967)	2000 normal	1	
Goodman, Smith & Migeon (1967)	100 prisoners of height 73" or over.	2	
Griffiths, and Zaremba, (1967)	34 prisoners of height 6' or over.	2	6 additional subjects exhibited other chromosomal anomalies.
	33 randomly selected prisoners.	0	5 subjects exhibited other chromo-somal anomalies.
Welch, Borgaonkar & Herr (1967)	11 delinquents height 6' or over. I.Q.<75.	0	
	12 most aggressive, defective delinquents of an institution.	0	
	22 defective delinquents of height 74" or over.	1	Epileptic. High plasma testosterone.

* For further details see Table I at end of paper.

Source	Population	XYY subjects	Special features
Telfer, Baker, Clark & Richardson (1968)	14 detained juvenile delinquents 5'11" or over.	1	
	30 detained adult mentally defective delinquents 5'11" or over.	0	
	35 detained adult delinquents 5'11" or over.	2	
	50 detained insane criminals 5'11" or over.	2	
Bartlett, Hurley, Brand & Poole (1968)	204 prisoners with non-certifiable psychiatric disorder.	2	Tall, schizoid personalities, homosexual. Convictions for arson. Moderate E.E.G. abnormalities.
Close, Goonetilleke, Jacobs & Price (1968)	19 institutionalised mentally subnormal patients 6' or over.	2	Both exhibited behaviour disturbances. 1 detained under court order.
	49 institutionalised mentally subnormal patients 5'10" - 5'11½".	0	
Court Brown (1968)	106 prisoners taller than 183 cm.	1	
	302 prisoners in allocation centre.	0	
	401 normal males over 6' tall.	0	
Hunter (1968)	29 Approved School inmates of top 10th percentile for height.	3	
Jacobs, Price & Court Brown (1968)	590 patients in hospital for the mentally subnormal.	0	
Wiener, Sutherland, Bartholomew & Hudson (1968)	34 prisoners of height 69" or over.	4 including 1 XYY-XYYY mosaic.	3 charged with murder or attempted murder. 2 below normal intelligence. 3 displayed abnormal E.E.G.
	300 retarded boys.	0	
	30 tall retarded adults.	0	

Source	Population	XYY subjects	Special features
Daly (1969)	210 tall inmates of maximum security hospitals.	10	High incidence of neurological abnormalities and body asymmetry.
Knox & Nevin (1969)	32 tall inmates of mental deficiency hospitals.	1	
Vanasek, Rucci & Thompson (1969)	67 prisoners of height 177.5 cm or over.	0	
	200 tall (6' or over) patients of a maximum security institution for mentally disordered sex offenders and the criminally insane.	9	Mentally disordered sex offenders 8.9 of sample. Criminally insane 1.6%
Walzer, Breau & Gerald (1969)	1931 newborn males.	0	
Jacobs et al., unpublished	607 admissions to borstals.	1	
	11 young offenders 183 cm. or over.	1	
Nielsen & Tsuboi (1969)	1180 patients in a mental hospital.	3	
	400 patients with personality deviation & criminality.	6	
Lubs & Ruddle (1969) Personal communication quoted in Ratcliffe et al. (1970)	2222 newborn males.	3	
Sergovich, Valentine, Chen, Kinch & Smouth (1969)	1066 consecutive newborn babies.	4	

Source	Population	XYY subjects	Special features
Akesson, Forssman & Wallin (1969)	117 tall (6' or over) patients of two psychiatric hospitals.	3 + 1 XYY/XY mosaic	1 persistent criminal with mental retardation and epilepsy. 2 diagnosed as prolonged neurotic syndrome, one being of below average intelligence and the other having attended a special class at school. 1 diagnosed as chronic psychosis. E.E.G. abnormal in 3 cases.
Ratcliffe, Stewart, Melville, Jacobs & Keay (1970)	3496 newborn males.	5	

dossiers, records of previous sentences, hospital and school reports. The ultimate sources of these additional media were imperfectly specified but included information, factual and speculative, obtained from the prisoner, his employers, relatives and other persons. It became apparent at an early stage that the reports contained many discrepancies, confined not only to subjective assessments, but including important factual data such as the number of children or age at first conviction. Prisoners themselves are not as a class over-concerned with veracity, and also tend to compensate in personal fantasies at the expense of reality. Although every effort was made to substantiate sociological variables, their statistical reliability is not assessable at this stage.

The following variables were studied in subjects and controls.

Sociological

Number of brothers and sisters and their relative incidence.
Birth order.
Education and employment level of criminal compared to that of brothers.
Family history of crime or serious alcoholism.
Parents' temperament and harmony.
Childhood happiness.
Childhood friends.
Prisoner's relationship to father, mother and siblings.
Abscondence and enforced separation from home in childhood.
Type of school and educational qualifications.
Favourite school subject.
Liking for school.
Truancy.
Expulsion from school.
Liking for games.
Favourite game.
Membership of school team.
Main occupation.
Other occupations.
Number of jobs.
Longest job.
Type of longest job.
Maximum earnings.
Reason for changing jobs.
Favourite job.
Drink pattern, amount, locality and age at onset.
Smoking.
Drugs, type.
Gambling.
Interests.
Amount of time spent out of home.
Usual companion when out of home.

Sociological (cont.)

Main indoor activity.
Importance of cars and driving.
Club membership.
Whether sports spectator.
Ability to mix.
Worries.
Future plans.
Sexual partnership, present and past.
Girl friends before marriage.
Children.

Criminal

Family history of crime.
Reason for offence.
Type of victim.
Prisoner's attitude to victim.
Degree of planning.
Degree of compulsiveness.
Age at first conviction.
Number of offences.
Number of times convicted.
Total period spent in prison.
Analysis of offences.

Medical

Height of criminal compared to that of father and brothers.
Familial diseases.
Family history of psychiatric disorder and serious alcoholism.
Parental ages at prisoner's birth.
Prisoner's medical and surgical history including accidents.
Prisoner's psychiatric history.

Subjects and controls received also a physical examination, and as many as possible underwent the following psychological tests:

(a) Wechsler Adult Intelligence Scale,
(b) Eysenck P.E.N. Questionnaire,
(c) Foulds and Caine Extrapunitive Intrapunitive Scale.

Results: Pair differences were evaluated by the Wilcoxon 2-tailed Signed Ranks Test. Differences at the .02 level of significance were found in respect of intelligence levels (Table III); and the extent of previous psychiatric history was ascertained (Table IV). The latter was estimated in numerical form by scoring each prisoner as follows:

History of psychiatric illness requiring institutional treatment   3
   "   "   "   "   "   only out-patient treatment 2
   "   "   untreated psychiatric disturbance   1
No history of psychiatric disturbance   0

Differences at the .05 level of significance were found in respect of the number of previous convictions (Table V); and a relative achievement scale is shown in Table VI, the latter being a simply calibrated numerical expression of each prisoner's scholastic achievement and employment level relative to his father and brothers. Differences approaching this level of significance were found in respect of the number of previous accidents, the sum of previous theft and breaking-in offences; and a sociability scale (Table VII) was composed of 8 questionnaire items bearing a substantial relationship to sociability, each item being scored as 0 in the direction of solitariness or 1 in the direction of sociability. This difference may be reflected in the extraversion scores of the P.E.N. questionnaire (Table VIII).

One subject and three controls had a family history of treated psychiatric disorder. Three subjects and four controls had near relatives who had been convicted of criminal offences. Severe alcoholism occurred in one or both parents (usually the father) in the case of seven subjects and two controls.

Four subjects, but none of the controls, attended schools for difficult or maladjusted children; this factor prevented exact comparison of educational levels per se. One subject and one control obtained the G.C.E. Four subjects and one control had a history of truancy; three subjects and one control had been expelled. All the controls recalled a liking for school games, these latter were, however, disliked by four of the subjects.

Any useful comparison of employment between subjects and controls was frustrated by their large number of jobs, the great variety of their nature and the considerable degree of discrepancy between the various records. There remained a strong impression, however, that the subjects' employment was in general considerably less skilled than that of the controls. The magnitude of the recorded discrepancies was also investigated but no significant differences were found between subjects and controls.

Two subjects and one control could be regarded as heavy drinkers; three subjects and two controls had taken drugs but none could be described as addicts. There were no serious gamblers in either group.

Six subjects and three controls had no established sexual partner. No subject or control professed homosexual tendencies but the latter appeared in the records of three of the subjects. Four subjects, but no controls, admitted having few or no girl-friends before marriage.

On physical examination, two subjects exhibited tremor, three nystagmoid movements and two stammer; such features were not apparent in the controls apart from one case of tremor. Two subjects had pes cavus, and one slight facial hemiatrophy.

Summary

An attempt was made to evaluate distinguishing features of the XYY constitution by comparing a group of such prisoners with their controls. The conclusions so far reached are necessarily somewhat weakened by the small number of subjects examined, the unassessed reliability of sociological data and the heterogeneity of controls; for these reasons the study is to be regarded more in the nature of a survey. Nevertheless, the impression was formed that the XYY constitution in prisoners may be accompanied by the following tendencies:

1. A past history of mental illness, often severe, and usually designated psychopathy.
2. Decreased intelligence.
3. Dilution of achievement in comparison with father and brothers.
4. Increased number of convictions but not of total offences.
5. Increased height in comparison with father and brothers.
6. A criminal history of offences against property.
7. Asocial personality.
8. Severe alcoholism of ascendants, usually father.
9. Homosexuality, covert rather than overt.

Their degree of interdependence must remain speculative at this stage, many more cases being desirable for satisfactory factorial analysis. However, the XYY constitution is considered to have achieved some measure of definition and it might be profitable to explore its biochemical aspects in greater detail.

Acknowledgments

The work has been supported by grants from the Mental Health Research Fund, the Home Office Research Unit and the South West Metropolitan Hospital Board. The psychological results were elaborated through the kind offices of Mr. Rudgard and other psychologists of the Prison Service. We are indebted to Miss I.H. Hollings for undertaking the secretarial work.

TABLE I

Previous cytogenetic surveys

(The word "prisoners" includes detained juvenile delinquents)

Sample	No.	XYY	%	References
Prisoners unselected	939	1	0.1	Court Brown (1968b); Griffiths & Zaremba (1967); Jacobs et al. (1969), personal communication.
tall	431	16	3.7	Casey et al. (1966a); Court Brown (1968b); Goodman et al. (1967); Hunter (1968); Jacobs et al. (1969), personal communication; Knox & Nevin (1969); Telfer et al. (1968); Welch et al. (1967); Wiener et al. (1968)
Criminals with psychiatric disorder (usually cared for in special institutions) unselected	931	17	1.8	Bartlett et al. (1968); Daly (1969b); Jacobs et al. (1965): Nielsen & Tsuboi (1969); Welch et al. (1967)
tall	612	38	6.2	Casey et al. (1966a); Daly (1969b); Telfer et al. (1968); Vanasek et al. (1969); Welch et al. (1967)
Psychiatric patients unselected	2070	3	0.1	Jacobs et al. (1968); Nielsen & Tsuboi (1969); Wiener et al. (1968)
tall	247	7	2.8	Akesson et al. (1969); Close et al. (1968); Daly (1969); Wiener et al. (1968)
General population	11116	13	0.1	Court Brown (1967b); Court Brown (1968); Lubs & Ruddle (1969), personal communication quoted in Ratcliffe et al. (1970); Ratcliffe et al. (1970); Sergovich et al. (1969); Walzer et al. (1969)

TABLE II

Incidence of karyotype 47 XYY

Sub-group	Specimens successfully cultured	Karyotype 47 XYY
I	34	2
II	31	1
III	290	6

TABLE III

Intelligence quotients

Pair No.	Verbal		Performance		Full Scale	
	XYY	Control	XYY	Control	XYY	Control
1	91	101	91	102	90	101
2	97	116	90	108	93	114
3	94	102	93	97	93	99
4	91	96	85	98	87	97
5	88	107	97	108	91	108
6	102	127	98	124	100	127
7	103	100	89	120	97	109

TABLE IV

Extent of previous psychiatric history

Pair No.	XYY	Control
1	3	1
2	1	0
3	2	0
4	1	1
5	3	2
6	3	2
7	2	0
8	3	1
9	1	1

It will be noted that 4 subjects but no controls had received treatment in mental hospitals.

TABLE V

Mean values

	XYY	Controls
Number of siblings	2.9	3.3
Birth order	2.5	2.6
Paternal age at prisoner's birth (years)	33	30.3
Maternal age at prisoner's birth (years)	28	25.8
Number of jobs	16.1	11.4
Longest job (months)	22.1	22.8
Maximum weekly earnings (pounds)	33.8	37.6
Number of serious accidents	1.3	0.4
Number of children	1.4	0.7
Age at first conviction (years)	16.7	16.1
Number of offences	31	34.5
Number of times convicted	13	9.2
Total length of previous sentences (months)	56	62.3
Number of offences by category:		
drink or drugs	0.3	0.2
fraud	0.3	14.8
theft	13.7	10.6
taking and driving away	2.8	2.3
breaking-in	4.8	3.0
violence (property)	0.4	0.2
violence (person)	0.3	0.8
sexual offences	0.3	0

Prisoners taller than father: 6 out of 7 subjects; 4 out of 7 controls.
Prisoners taller than brothers: 5 out of 5 subjects; 5 out of 8 controls.

TABLE VI

Achievement relative to father and brothers

Pair	XYY	Control
1	-1	+1
2	-2	+1
3	-1	0
5	-3	-2
6	-1	-1
7	-2	0
8	-1	-1
9	-1	0

TABLE VII

Sociability score

Pair	XYY	Control
1	3	7
2	0	6
3	4	6
4	7	7
5	2	5
6	5	7
7	5	5
8	0	4
9	5	3

TABLE VIII

Eysenck P.E.N. questionnaire

Control scores appear in parentheses

Pair	Psychoticism	Extraversion	Neuroticism
1	8 (9)	7 (13)	8 (6)
2	16 (5)	7 (14)	17 (4)
3	13 (13)	15 (17)	21 (7)
4	5 (16)	13 (14)	8 (16)
5	9 (3)	8 (16)	12 (15)

CHROMOSOME STUDIES IN REMAND HOME AND PRISON POPULATIONS

J. Kahn, W.I. Carter*, N. Dernley[†], and E.T.O. Slater

Introduction

Price and Whatmore (1967a) described behaviour disorders in 9 XYY males, all of whom were identified at a maximum security hospital. They found that the mean age at first conviction for the XYY males was 13.1 years, whereas the mean age at first conviction in the control group was 18 years. The difference in the means was significant at the 5% level. In addition, at least 5 of the 9 XYY males had been in trouble with education authorities and the police on account of minor offences or persistent truancy from school. It was for these reasons that we decided to undertake a cytogenetical investigation of young offenders.

Material and Methods

During weekly visits over a period of two years we collected 387 samples from Stamford House Remand Home, 200 samples from the Borstal Wing of Wormwood Scrubs and 128 samples from women in Holloway Prison. The latter constituted part of a larger random sample used in a sociological study in Professor Gibbens' department at the Institute of Psychiatry. Blood was only taken after permission had been given in writing. No criteria other than parental consent and availability were used in choosing boys and it can be assumed that we had a random sample. Boys under care and protection were excluded from this study.

Date of birth and height were taken at the time of our visit to the remand home. Owing to administrative difficulties, height was not obtained consistently either for the borstal boys or for the Holloway women.

Peripheral blood was processed for chromosomes in the usual way, based on a method by Moorhead and co-workers (1960). Unless otherwise mentioned, 10 cells were analysed per individual. Cytogenetic abnormalities and anomalies were defined and recorded in the following manner:

I. **Chromosome abnormalities**

 (1) Consistent trisomy; presence of an extra chromosome in all the analysed cells of an individual.

 (2) Consistent structural rearrangements of chromosomes in all the analysed cells of an individual.

 (3) Mosaicism, where more than one cell type was found and where we had reason to believe that this was not due to culture artefacts.

II. **Chromosome polymorphism**

 (4) Individuals with Y chromosomes consistently equal or larger than F chromosomes, or with Y consistently smaller than G chromosomes (marker Y chromosomes).

 (5) Individuals with an autosome which always deviated slightly in size or shape from its homologue (marker autosomes).

---

* General Practitioner, visiting Medical Officer, Stamford House and Wormwood Scrubs

[†] Medical Research Council Clinical Genetics Unit, Institute of Child Health

TABLE

Anomalies	Stamford House (387)			Wormwood Scrubs (200)			Holloway (128)		
	Obs.	Exp.	Signif.	Obs.	Exp.	Signif.	Obs.	Exp.	Signif.
Percentile height:									
≤ 25	157	97							
50	168	193							
> 75	62	97							
Chromosome:									
Trisomy	3	†<1	?	2	**<0.5	Sig.	0	–	–
Autosomal rearrangements	3	†2	Nil	1	?	?	2	†<1	?
Mosaicism	3	?	?				0	–	–
D	12	*2.0	p<0.001	7	*1.0	p<0.01	1	*0.7	Nil
E	4	*3.6	Nil	1	*1.8	Nil	1	*1.2	Nil
G	7	*3.0	Nil	3	*1.6	Nil	5	*1.0	0.020>p>0.01
Y long	18	*7.0	0.05>p>0.025	5	*3.6	Nil	–	–	–
Y short	3	*3.0	Nil	2	*1.5	Nil	–	–	–
TOTAL NUMBER INVESTIGATED	387			200			128		

* Calculated from Court Brown *et al.* (1966).

** 1.2% general population

† Based on estimate from Court Brown *et al.* (1966).

(These morphological variations have been described by Court Brown *et al.* (1966).*

Results

The distribution of heights of the remand home boys showed signs of a general shift to the left. Instead of 25% only 16% of the boys were on or above the 75th percentile of school boys of their ages (Tanner's standard), and 40.6% were below the 25th percentile.

I. Chromosome abnormalities

 a) Stamford House Remand Home (9 boys)

 (1) Trisomy: Two boys had an XYY sex-chromosome constitution; as expected they were above the 75th percentile for height. Their parents had normal chromosomes. One boy had an additional metacentric element in all the cells examined. This chromosome of unknown origin was smaller than the F chromosomes.

 (2) Structural rearrangements: One boy carried a balanced DqDq translocation inherited from his mother. In addition he had a marker G chromosome inherited from his father. One boy had a possible translocation between the short arms of a G and a D chromosome resulting in Gp+; Dp-. (The parents were not investigated in this case; therefore this interpretation must be viewed with reservation.)
 One boy had a short G autosome (of the G$^{'Ph'}$ type).

 (3) Mosaicism: Three boys below the 25th percentile had XO/XY mosaicism. Two of these boys had 4XO and 26 XY cells; the third boy had 7 XO and 23 XY cells.

 b) Wormwood Scrubs (2 + 1? boys)

 (1) Trisomy: Two boys were XYY Klinefelters.

 (2) & (3) Structural rearrangement and mosaicism: One boy was a possible mosaic for a deleted D chromosome, 3Dq-cells and 32 normal cells.

 c) Holloway (2 women)

 (1) Trisomy: None.

 (2) Structural rearrangement: One woman had a DqGq centric fusion type of translocation. One woman had a possible Dp-Gp+ interchange rearrangement similar to that found in a Stamford House boy. (No information on the parents' chromosomes was available.)

 (3) Mosaicism: None.

II. Chromosome polymorphism

 a) Stamford House Remand Home

 (4) Y chromosomes: 18 Yq+; 3 Yq-.

 (5) Autosomes: 12 Dp+; 4 Eq+; 7 Gp+.

* Doubtful markers were not included in the analysis; in a proportion of cases our observations were checked independently by Dr. J.L. Hamerton or a member of his group at the Paediatric Research Unit at Guy's Hospital.

b) Wormwood Scrubs

    (4) Y chromosomes: 5 Yq+; 2 Yq-.

    (5) Autosomes: 8 Dp+; 1 Eq+; 3 Gp+.
        One boy had two distinguishable Dp+ chromosomes.

c) Holloway

    (4) None.

    (5) Autosomes: 1 Dp+; 1 Eq+; 5 Gp+.

Discussion

Our Stamford House sample of 387 boys yielded 2 cases with an XYY constitution. Only 16% of this population were of a height on or above the 75th percentile and since we expect to find XYY cases almost exclusively in this range, our finding becomes still more significant when expressed as 2 XYY/60 XY (boys ≥ 75th percentile).

Our figure of 2 XYY/385 XY is not significantly different from the figure given by Court Brown and Smith (1969) who found 1 XYY/606 XY in Scottish borstals. The majority of XYY cases reported in the literature were discovered as a result of studying special populations, prisons, borstals and hospitals. Therefore no true estimate of their frequency in the general population is available, but Court Brown's estimate (1968b) of 0.1% XYY in the new-born population can be adopted as a guide line until further information on adult populations is obtained.

A frequency of two cases of Klinefelter's syndrome (XXY) in a sample of 200 borstal boys is statistically significant (0.12% in the general population, $p = 0.0245$).

The finding of 4 mosaics (3 Stamford House, 1? Wormwood Scrubs) must be regarded as an underestimate for two reasons: (1) the limited number of cells analysed per individual; (2) the fact that blood was the only tissue examined. Nevertheless we believe that the 3 XO/XY from Stamford House are of special interest, not the least because of their short stature. This result also emphasises the importance of studying a cross-section of a population and not confining oneself to tall boys. The boy mosaic for a deleted D chromosome (Wormwood Scrubs) may be of particular interest because in a sporadic case which we have investigated (on the request of one of H.M. Prisons) the patient, with a grossly aberrant behaviour pattern, had a deleted D chromosome in all his cells.

The number of autosomal rearrangements was in agreement with the findings of Court Brown and co-workers (1966). However, in future work special attention should be given to finding ways and means for objectively identifying minor translocations of the Dp-, Gp+ and similar types. Such translocations may play a role in the aetiology of some marker chromosomes. This also underlines the desirability of family studies wherever possible in an attempt to diagnose the origin of these anomalies. It is conceivable that a DDp-, GGp+ in a parent could result in DDp-, GG and DD, GGp+ in his or her offspring.

The importance of these studies is further stressed by the finding of a significant excess of Dp+ in male offenders as against a significant excess of Gp+ amongst female offenders. Of the 12 Stamford House boys with Dp+ marker chromosomes, 9 were of a height below the 25th percentile. This distribution is just significant with $p < 0.05$.

There was a marked excess of long Y chromosomes in the Stamford House sample ($0.05 > p > 0.025$), but only a small excess in the Wormwood Scrubs sample. The difference between these two samples is far from significant ($0.30 > p > 0.20$). As there is no reason to think that the two groups of boys should differ from one another in respect of their Y chromosomes, the two samples may be combined. The frequency of long Y's in the combined group of 587, namely 3.9%, is more than twice as great as in Court Brown's controls (1.8%), and the difference is significant ($0.05 > p > 0.04$).

Neither group showed an excess of short Y chromosomes. There was no correlation between the long Y chromosomes and height in the Stamford House sample; this suggests that if the increase in size was due to duplication of the chromosome's own genetic material, it did not involve the segment which carries genes for height.

In this study the difference between male and female offenders with regard to marker chromosomes was significant.

In conclusion, we think that future chromosome studies should not focus solely on anomalies of the sex chromosomes; and furthermore we think that selection for height is not desirable in such studies.

Acknowledgments

This work was carried out while J.K., N.D. and E.T.O.S. were on the staff of the Medical Research Council Psychiatric Genetics Unit, Institute of Psychiatry.

We are grateful to the Home Office Prison Department (Medical Services) for allowing us to carry out this survey. We should like to thank the Managing Committee of Stamford House for their co-operation and their superintendent, Mr. Clifford Heap: the medical staff of all three institutions, Dr. P.D. Scott, Psychiatrist, and the nursing staff at Stamford House, the Principal Medical Officers and nursing staff at Wormwood Scrubs and Holloway Prisons, Professor T.C.N. Gibbens and Mrs. Joyce Prince for arranging access to their sample of Holloway prisoners. We are especially indebted to those inmates of Stamford House, Wormwood Scrubs and Holloway Prisons who volunteered blood samples for our study.

THE FAMILY AND BEHAVIOURAL HISTORY OF PATIENTS WITH CHROMOSOME ABNORMALITY IN THE SPECIAL HOSPITALS OF RAMPTON AND MOSS SIDE

M.D. Casey

Introduction

The subject of this paper is a review of various factors in the family history of patients from the special hospitals of Rampton and Moss Side. A number of comparisons have been made between the families of patients with chromosome abnormality and control groups in a search for any significant differences between the two, and for differences between these families and the general population.

My background to this work is a general medical one with some specialised knowledge of genetics. In the paper which follows therefore, I have not attempted to make any psychiatric interpretation of the various factors concerned, but merely confined myself to a comparison and to the genetic aspects.

Study populations

The patients concerned are (a) 33 with an XYY chromosome constitution (22 at Rampton and 11 at Moss Side), (b) 21 XXY (16 at Rampton and 5 at Moss Side), (c) 9 XXYY (5 at Rampton and 4 at Moss Side), and (d) 150 randomly selected controls (50 at Rampton and 100 at Moss Side). The controls were randomly selected and not matched for age, I.Q., date of admission, diagnosis or other factor.

Source of information

Information about the families was obtained from hospital case notes, letters to schools, to medical officers of health and from home visits. In some cases it is necessarily incomplete or unreliable, due to retrospective collection; but an attempt has been made to assess this for various parameters. Any errors for ascertainment should be the same for each group of patients once any obvious sources of bias have been excluded. For example, family background is obviously more difficult to obtain in the case of older patients, or patients with unco-operative families, and if one group contained an undue proportion of these then this would bias the results; this, however, was not found in our data.

Factors studied

The family background of the patients was investigated under the following main headings:

1. General family background: illegitimacy, parental age, birth order, family size.

2. Social background: occupation and social class of father and of patient.

3. Factors which might distort, disrupt, or cause discontinuity in the upbringing of the patient to indicate a disturbed family background.
   (a) Death of parent/sib.
   (b) Physical illness of parent/sib.
   (c) Mental illness of parent/sib.
   (d) Subnormality of parent/sib.
   (e) Desertion or divorce of parents.

4. Other factors in the early history which might lead to faulty

development: criminality in the rest of the family; serious illness of patient.

Source and Purpose of Factors

Some of these factors are specifically of genetic interest as indicating the incidence of some condition in first-degree relatives (parent/sib.), or the origin of the aneuploid state (parental age effect). Others are of more psychiatric interest and are taken from the work of Dr John Bowlby in his monograph to the World Health Organisation on maternal deprivation as a cause of disturbed and retarded behaviour.[1] As I have previously said I am not making any statement about the precise effect of any of these factors, the results of many of which are controversial, but am confining myself to a comparison between patients with chromosome abnormality, controls and the general population.

Illegitimacy

The first factor to be investigated was illegitimacy. The figures are shown in Table I. The illegitimacy rate in the general population was about 5% over the period during which these patients were born.[2] The figure for the special hospital control groups was 15%, significantly higher at the 1% level. This is to be expected since illegitimate children whose parents are of subcultural mental level are preferentially selected for institutional care.[3]

The illegitimacy rate for XYY patients is also 15% which is again significantly higher than that in the general population (P - 0.01). In contrast there were no illegitimates among the patients with an extra X chromosome, XXY or XXYY. This is not significantly different from the figure expected in the general population, but is significantly less at the 5% level than the percentage observed in the special hospitals. It is possible that this observation is related to the increased parental age of people with this karyotype (Penrose, 1964). The illegitimacy rate falls off sharply after the age of 21 and continues to drop with advancing maternal age;[4] since the mean maternal age of XXY patients is over 30 this is one explanation for the findings.

Parental age

The effects of parental age were next looked for. There were no significant differences in mean parental age between XYY, Special Hospital controls and the general population (Table II). Patients with an XXY chromosome constitution had a significant increase in both maternal and paternal age as would be expected from what is known of their karyotype.

Birth rank and family size

Finally in this section effects of birth rank and family size were investigated. There were no significant differences in birth order (Table III) between patients with chromosome abnormality, controls and the general population except in the case of patients with the XXY karyotype. These, as expected, were born significantly later in their sibships than either the remainder of the special hospital patients or the average for

[1] Bowlby, J. *Maternal care and mental health*, 2nd ed., 1952. Geneva: World Health Organization, monog. series, no.2.
[2] *Registrar General's statistical review of England and Wales for the year 1965*, Part II, Tables, population, p.136. London: H.M.S.O.
[3] Penrose, L.S. *The biology of mental defect*, p.63. London: Sidgwick & Jackson, 3rd ed., 1963.
[4] *Reg.-General's statistical review...1965*, Part II, p.136.

the general population.

It can be seen from Table III that XXY, XYY and control patients come from families of above average size. Size of sibship is known to be inversely correlated with intelligence and this observation suggests that the aneuploid patients in the special hospitals are born into families somewhat less intelligent than the average. The means cannot be directly compared with the mean for the general population of 2.2 as the special hospital families are selected by the presence of at least one child.[5]

Social Class and Socio-Economic Group

Further data to support this observation are found when social class and socio-economic group are investigated. It was possible to classify occupation of the father at birth of the patient on the basis of social class and socio-economic group in the Registrar-General's returns of 1961; these are shown in Table IV.

The observed numbers of fathers in the five different categories of social class based on general standing in the community differ significantly from expectation except in the case of XXY and XXYY patients. Expected numbers are based on the figures from the whole community in the 1961 census.[6] The deviation from expectation is due to the over-representation of fathers in social classes IV and V (partly skilled and unskilled) and their under-representation in categories I, II and III (professional, intermediate and skilled).

The socio-economic groups contain people whose social, cultural and recreational standards are the same. Again, observed numbers deviate significantly from expectation except in the case of XXY and XXYY patients. This seems to be due largely to the excess of semi-skilled and unskilled manual workers and, in the case of controls, of agricultural workers. The relevant proportion in these different occupations are not thought to have changed significantly since the 1939 census.

Factors leading to disturbed family background

Some others factors in the family background, more specifically related to the upbringing of the patient, were next considered. They were separated first into those factors which affected either or both parents and thus might lead to parental deprivation or some form of distortion or discontinuity in the upbringing, and second into those that were present in siblings as well. The presence of mental illness, subnormality or criminality in a sibling even if the parents were both apparently normal might suggest some familial predisposition.

Table V shows the results of the investigation with respect to three specific factors, (a) loss or absence of parent for six months or more before the age of six years, (b) convictions in parents or siblings and (c) mental illness or mental subnormality in parents or siblings. It is in this part of the investigation that problems of ascertainment become prominent; in many cases it is not possible to obtain full information about the family. The degree of ascertainment may be estimated by comparing the proportion in each category found by reference to hospital case notes with the proportion found by personal interview with the patient's family or from some other source. It was possible to do this in the case of the Rampton patients, almost all these families being interviewed; information about the Moss Side controls was obtained entirely from hospital case notes.

[5] Penrose, L.S. *The biology of mental defect,* p.58.
[6] *Census 1961, England & Wales. Occupation tables,* pp.195-9. London: H.M.S.O.

This table requires a little more explanation than the others. Parental absence for six months or more for any cause before six years refers to a true loss of the putative parent. In almost every case in which this happened in the scored categories this seems to have led to the breaking-up of the home, or to have been a sequel to a disturbed home environment. It probably under-represents the true figure. Three illegitimates are not scored because they were brought up by foster parents from birth. In a number of unscored cases information was unobtainable. The columns in which total figures are given are not mutually exclusive - in a number of cases with parental absence, for example, there may have been convicted members of the family as well and in such a case the family is scored as one.

(a) Parental absence

The most unexpected result of this part of the investigation as seen in Table V is the relative lack of difference between the various categories of patient. In the case of parental absence approximately one third of controls, one third of patients with an XYY karyotype and one third of those with an XXY karyotype had lost either father or mother before the age of six years. There was no significant difference in this figure depending on whether case notes or interview was the source of the information. It almost certainly under-represents the true figure, however, for in a number of cases no information could be obtained about the patient's early life. When cause of parental absence is broken down into the three categories, death, illegitimacy or desertion, again approximately the same proportions are seen.

(b) Convictions

The proportion of patients with convictions in other members of the family was also similar in the various groups. This scoring was made on the basis of presence or absence of a conviction and not on the number of convictions per sibling, which might not be available. The relative proportion is similar in the three groups in Rampton and Moss Side, but the absolute proportion is considerably less in Moss Side than in Rampton, approximately 10% and 30% respectively. This difference is considered to be due to ascertainment. By reference to Rampton Hospital case notes, only three of the 22 patients with an XYY karyotype were recorded as having a criminal history in siblings or parents; after interview, the proportion went up to 8/22.

This finding in both hospitals of a similar proportion of families with convictions in both XYY patients and controls is in contrast to that of the Edinburgh group at Carstairs (Price & Whatmore, 1967a).

(c) Mental illness or subnormality

The final comparison in this section, proportion of families with a mentally ill or mentally subnormal parent or sibling, shows a similar high proportion in all groups. Again, however, the proportion is less in Moss Side than in Rampton; again perhaps because of ascertainment. Mental illness was defined as attendance at a mental hospital or in-patient residence for a period. Mental subnormality was similarly defined as attendance at an E.S.N. school or occupation centre, or registration as a mental defective. In this section no scoring was made on the basis of personal impressions by an interviewer, such as "parents of low intellect" or "of disturbed personality". Such judgments although probably valid could not be considered comparable unless all made by the same observer, and by an observer who did not know the karyotype of the patient.

In these latter two categories, criminality and mental illness or subnormality, a sibling is more commonly affected than a parent. The presence of these categories in siblings does suggest some familial predisposition other than chromosome abnormality.

Comparison of offences of patients with those of their families

Those patients in Rampton with a family history of convictions were looked at in a little more detail to ascertain if the extra chromosome made any striking difference in behaviour. Table VI shows some of these observations. These patients tended to fall into the same diagnostic classes with respect to Mental Health Act classification as the remainder of their respective groups. There was no undue proportion of severely subnormal, or patients with psychopathic disorder in this group. They tended to commit the same type of offence as the family, sometimes being charged jointly with a sibling. However, there was an increased proportion of sexual offences in patients compared with their family: of the XYY patients 3/8 were convicted of sexual offences compared with 1/8 of their families; of the XXY's 7/10 as compared with 1/10, and of controls 6/15 as compared with 3/15.

Discussion

The results of family studies in the two Special Hospitals seem to show a consistent pattern. Over half the families in the three groups, XYY, XXY, and controls, have a familial incidence of either disturbed behaviour, mental disorder or parental loss. The surprising feature of these results is the similar incidence of these factors in patients with chromosome abnormality and controls. If it is an extra chromosome which predisposes to disturbed behaviour, it would be expected that these patients would have a relatively smaller incidence of these factors in the family. It was possible to show in 20 families that the chromosome abnormality has arisen *de novo* as a mutation and is not familial; this is to be expected from what is known of these aneuploid states. Patients with an XXYY karyotype had a lower familial incidence of convictions, mental disorder, or parental absence, but the difference was not significant.

The results of studies on illegitimacy, family size and occupational status of patients suggest that patients of the Special Hospitals tend to come from the lower social groups and from families with a more disturbed background. Patients with chromosome abnormality seem to fall into the same pattern, suggesting that it is only a proportion of these patients who are seen in the Special Hospitals, a large number remaining in the rest of the population. This is certainly the case for the XXY karyotype, in which it is known from newborn and adult surveys that the number in the general population is very large (Maclean *et al.*, 1964). Some recent newborn chromosome-surveys suggest that the XYY state may be similarly common and if this proves to be the case then this would account for our findings (Sergovich *et al.*, 1969; Court Brown, 1968b). These results contrast with the findings at Carstairs where patients with an XYY karyotype tended to come from families with less convictions than controls (Price & Whatmore, 1967a).

A number of explanations for these differences are possible, all rather speculative. Ascertainment may have been incomplete at Carstairs, though this seems unlikely as an explanation for the differences, as controls would be expected to be as incompletely ascertained as XYY. Secondly, the number of controls and XYY patients is rather small; the probability that two groups with an incidence of some factor of 1/9 and 7/18 come from the same population is 15% when the family is considered as a unit. Thirdly, there may be a factor of selection to the different hospitals; there are less Special Hospital beds per head of population in England and Wales than in Scotland. It is possible that Rampton and Moss Side have a more disturbed type of patient coming from a more disturbed background; however, this difference should be apparent in the controls. Further studies on XYY families in subnormality hospitals of England and Wales not needing special security should clarify this.

The results of this work serve to show that the presence of an extra chromosome *per se* plays only a small part in predisposing to delinquency. Confirmation of this observation will require a great deal of prospective work from chromosome surveys of the newborn, but until this has been done it would seem premature to allow the presence of extra X or Y chromosomes to be used in legal proceedings.

Acknowledgments

I wish to thank Dr. J.M. McDougall of Moss Side Hospital, for permission to study his patients, and also Dr. C.E. Blank and the staff of the Department of Human Genetics, Sheffield, for their work and helpful comments.

TABLE I

Illegitimacy

About $4\frac{1}{2}\%$ in the general population from 1920 to 1940, about $5\frac{1}{2}\%$ since 1947.

Rampton	Proportion Illegitimate
Controls	7/50
XYY	4/22
XXY	0/16
XXYY	0/5
XXY/XY	0/2

Moss Side

Controls	15/100
XYY	1/11
XXY	0/5
XXYY	0/4
XXY/XY	1/1

Total

Controls	22/150
XYY	5/33
XXY	0/21
XXYY	0/9
XXY/XY	1/3

Carstairs

XYY	0/9
Controls	0/18

56

TABLE II

Parental Age

	N	Maternal Age	N	Paternal Age
General Population		28.47 (1939)		31.39 (1939)
Rampton				
XYY	20	26.6	19	29.4
XXY	15	33.60	16	36.70
XXYY	5	34.2	5	35.60
Controls		28.32		31.76
Moss Side				
XYY	6	26.2	5	34.2
XXY	5	29.5	5	33.5
XXYY	4	26.1	3	26.2
Totals				
XYY	26	26.6	24	30.4
XXY	20	32.6	21	36.0
XXYY	9	30.6	8	32.2
Controls				
Carstairs				
XYY	9	28.1	9	30.9

TABLE   III

Birth Rank and Family Size

	Birth Rank	N	Family Size	N
General Population	2.42		2.2	
Rampton				
XYY	2.8/5	21	5.05	21
XXY	4.00	15	5.70	15
XXYY	1.6	5	3.4	5
Controls	2.8/4.7	32	4.7	32
Moss Side				
XYY	3.7	8	5.7	8
XXY	2.4	5	5.0	5
XXYY	1.7	4	5.0	4
Controls			4.12	
Totals				
XYY	3.1	29	5.24	29
XXY	3.6	20	5.5	20
XXYY	1.7	9	4.1	9
Controls				

TABLE IV

Group	Socio-Economic Group	Expected No's. %	XYY		XXY		XXYY		Controls	
			Obs.	Exp.	Obs.	Exp.	Obs.	Exp.	Obs.	Exp.
1	Employers and managers – large establishments	3.6	0	0.9	0	0.8	0	0.3	2	4.1
2	Employers and managers – small establishments	5.9	0	1.5	1	1.2	0	0.5	0	6.7
3	Professional workers – self-employed	0.8	0	0.2	0	0.2	0	0.1	0	1.0
4	Professional workers – employees	3.0	0	0.8	0	0.7	0	0.3	3	0.4
5	Intermediate non-manual workers	3.9	0	1.0	0	0.9	0	0.4	1	4.4
6	Junior non-manual workers	12.6	0	3.3	0	2.6	0	1.1	3	14.2
7	Personal service workers	0.9	0	0.2	0	0.2	0	0.2	1	1.0
8	Foremen and supervisors – manual	3.3	0	0.8	0	0.7	0	0.3	0	3.7
9	Skilled manual workers	31.6	6	8.2	10	6.6	3	2.8	34	35.7
10	Semi-skilled manual workers	14.7	9	3.8	1	3.1	3	1.3	17	16.6
11	Unskilled manual workers	8.3	6	2.2	7	1.7	2	0.7	35	9.4
12	Own-account workers (other than professional)	3.4	2	0.9	1	0.7	1	0.3	2	3.8
13	Farmers – employers and managers	1.0	0	0.3	0	0.2	0	0.1	0	1.1
14	Farmers – own account	1.0	0	0.3	0	0.2	0	0.1	1	1.1
15	Agricultural workers	2.0	1	0.6	0	0.4	0	0.2	14	2.6
16	Members of the armed forces	2.0	2	0.5	1	0.4	0	0.2	0	2.6
17	Occupation inadequately described	1.7	0	0.4	0	0.3	0	0.2	0	2.2
	Social Class 1961									
I	Professional	3.9	0	1.0	0	0.2	0	0.3	3	4.4
II	Intermediate	14.4	1	3.7	0	3.0	0	1.3	7	16.3
III	Skilled	49.8	13	13	10	9.5	4	4.5	37	56.5
IV	Partly skilled	19.9	13	5.2	2	3.8	3	1.8	32	22.6
V	Unskilled	8.6	5	2.2	7	1.6	2	0.8	34	9.7

TABLE V

	1. Parental absence for 6 months or more, for any cause before 6 years.	Death of parent	Illegitimacy	Desertion	Other reasons	2. Parent/sib. with convictions	Parental absence and/or family convictions	3. Parent/sib. mental illness or subnormality	Total parental absence and/or family convictions or mental disorder
Rampton									
Controls	17/50	4/50	6/50	7/50	0/50	16/50 (8/50 parent)	23/50	14/50 (2/50 parent)	28/50
XYY	12/22	2/22	4/22	3/22	3/22*	8/22 (2/22 parent)	15/22	7/22 (3/22 parent)	18/22
XXY	7/16	3/16	0/16	2/16	2/16	10/16 (2/16 parent)	12/16	7/16 (3/16 parent)	12/16
XXYY	0/5	0/5	0/5	0/5	0/5 *nature of parents' employment	1/5	1/5	0/5	1/5
Moss Side									
Controls	32/100	8/100	13/100	10/100	1/100 Hospl. treatmt.	12/100 (7/100parent)	37/100	23/100 (13/100 parent)	52/100
XYY	5/11	1/11	1/11	3/11		1/11 (1/11 father)	6/11	1/11 parent	6/11
XXY	0/6					1/6	1/6	1/6	1/6
XXYY	1/4	1/4				0/4	1/4	1/4	1/4

TABLE VI

Rampton - Patient and Family Convictions

XYY

Hosp. No.	Convictions (patient)	Convictions (family)	Mental health classification
3335	2 + 3	2	P.D.
3443	2	2	S.S.
3425	2	2 + 3	S
3519	2	2	P.D.
3218	1	2	S
2901	1 + 2 + 3	2	S
3450	1 + 2	1 + 2	S
3463	2 + 3	2	S

XYY

Hosp. No.	Convictions (patient)	Convictions (family)	Mental health classification
3252	2	2	S
3273	1 + 2	2	S.S.
3288	1 + 2	2	S.S.
2887	2	2	S
3263	1 + 2	2	P.D.
3241	2 + 3	3	S
3408	2 + 3	2	P.D.
3579	2		P.D.
3440	2 + 3	1	P.D.
2847	1 + 2 + 3		S
3580	1 + 2	2	S

Controls

Hosp. No.	Convictions (patient)	Convictions (family)	Mental health classification
3454	1 + 2	2	P.D.
3123	2	2	S.S.
3282	1 + 2 + 3	2 + 3	S
3496	2 + 3	2	S.S.
3211	2	2	S
3429	1 + 2	2	S
3155	3	1	S
2911	1 + 2 + 3	1 + 3	P.D.
3167	1 + 2		S
1079	2		P.D.
3584	1 + 2	2	P.D.
2835	2		P.D.
3089	2 + 3	3	S.S.
2969	3	2	S.S.
3246	2	1 + 2	S

1 = Sexual offences
2 = Offences against property
3 = Offences against the person

PATIENTS WITH CHROMOSOME ABNORMALITIES IN
RAMPTON HOSPITAL: A REPORT

D.R.K. Street and R.A. Watson

Source of the Data

Rampton Hospital is one of the three Special Hospitals specifically designated as such under the provision of 1959 Mental Health Act for the care of patients of dangerous, violent or criminal propensities. The male side of the hospital is divided into two areas: the more secure area consists of 8 wards in the main building based on the old block system, and a less secure area of 10 villas for patients who are considered to have become more stable and less of a security risk. About 100 of the patients work during the day outside the security area but still within hospital grounds. As a patient becomes more stable, he progresses from one area to the other and so this provides some indication of behavioural change.

During the period 1967/68, a chromosome survey of all male patients in the hospital was carried out by the Department of Genetics at Sheffield University. The type and frequency of abnormality found is shown in Table 1.

TABLE 1

Incidence of chromosome abnormalities

	Rampton	General population
XYY	22 (3.38%)	0.14%
XXY	16 (2.4%)	0.2%
XXYY	5 (0.007%)	-
XXY/XY	2 (0.003%)	-

The findings reported here are based on three different studies carried out at three different periods of time and therefore involve three different groups of subjects.

In 1967, Little investigated some of the psychological characteristics of patients with an XYY chromosome structure. (At that time there were 17 such patients in the hospital.) He compared their performance on various tests (questionnaires) with those of a random sample of the Rampton population. A second control group was matched on age and length of stay at Rampton, and WAIS Verbal I.Q. was also used.

In 1968, McKerracher studied the behavioural characteristics of the XXY group of patients (16 present in the hospital at that time). He compared the social backgrounds, I.Q.s and galvanic skin responses of this group with that of a random sample of 96 male patients and a second control group of 14 patients matched on age and intelligence (McKerracher & Street, 1968).

Recently, a retrospective study was made of the offence patterns and hospital behaviour of all those patients with chromosomal abnormalities (45 patients). Similar information was obtained for a random sample of the hospital population. A detailed physical examination was also carried out on patients of the index group who were still in the hospital (26 patients).

Results

Preadmission data

There is considerable variation in the consistency of the information available in the Hospital Case Notes. Data most consistently and reliably available relate to past court experiences. It should be mentioned that, by the time the patients arrive at Rampton, most of them have had a very varied career which includes offences against both property and the person. Table 2 attempts to summarise some features of their behaviour.

TABLE 2

Preadmission data

	XYY (N=22)	Controls (N=50)	XXY (N=16)
Mean age of first conviction	15.8	16.2	15.7
Types of offences committed:			
Against the person (sexual)	13 (59%)	17 (34%)	9 (56%)
Against the person (non-sexual)	12 (55%)	29 (58%)	8 (50%)
Against property (with violence)	3 (14%)	8 (16%)	4 (25%)
Against property (minus violence)	15 (68%)	30 (60%)	10 (63%)
Behaviour immediately prior to admission:			
Aggression to person (non-sex)	7 (32%)*	29 (58%)	6 (37%)*
Indecent assault on male	3 (14%)	1 (2%)	2 (13%)
Indecent assault on female	6 (27%)	9 (18%)	3 (18%)
Property offence	1 (4%)	3 (6%)	1 (6%)
Absconding from hospital	0 (0%)	2 (4%)	2 (13%)
Others	5 (27%)	6 (12%)	2 (13%)

* significant at < .05

It is apparent that on the majority of factors the three groups are very similar. When all past offences are considered, then there are no significant differences between the groups in respect of broad categories of offences. However, if only the events immediately prior to admission to hospital are considered (including pieces of behaviour not resulting in prosecution), then the XYY patients show significantly fewer aggressive acts against the person (p<.02). The XXY group also shows significantly fewer aggressive acts against the person.

McKerracher also noted that the XXY group had committed fewer heterosexual offences than his controls, which confirmed a similar finding by other workers (Casey *et al.*, 1968), had used violence to a less extent in the perpetration of other crimes, and more commonly had a history of absconding from other institutions before coming to Rampton.

Admission data

Information relating to age on admission, source and Mental Health Act classification is shown in Table 3.

TABLE 3
Admission data

	XYY (N=22)	Controls (N=50)	XXY (N=16)
Admission source:		.	
hospital	10 (45%)	27 (54%)	7 (41%)
courts	12 (55%)	19 (38%)	9 (59%)
prison	0	4 (8%)	0
Mean age on admission:	23.1 years	25.6 years	29.3 years
Classification:			
Psychopathic disorder	12 (55%)**	171 (25%)	4 (25%)
Subnormality	6 (27%)	260 (38%)	10 (62%)
Severe subnormality	4 (18%)	192 (28%)	2 (13%)
Other	0	63 (9%)	0

** significant at < .01

The XYY group are younger than the control group on admission; the XXY group rather older. Slightly more of those with chromosomal abnormalities had come directly from the court whereas the control groups tended more often to come from another institution (hospital or prison). Psychopathic disorder was most frequently listed as primary diagnosis for the XYY group (significantly more so than in the other two groups, p<.01). In both the XYY and XXY groups, there are fewer patients recorded as being severely subnormal although the difference is not significant.

Physical examination

The study by Little confirmed previous findings for a tendency in patients with an XYY structure to be of increased stature.

TABLE 4
Physical examination (a)

	XYY	Controls	XXY
Height (mean):	71.33"	67.37"	68.25"
Body build:	Mesomorphic	Endomorphic	N.K.
Tattoos:	13.6%	15.4%	18.7%

The XYY group was found to be significantly taller than the control group at the 1% level of confidence. Although the XYY group was not uniformly tall, 9 out of 17 were over 6ft in height (53%) as compared with 2 of the 17 controls (12%).

Little also used the Rees-Eysenck Body Index. Two measurements are used in the construction of this index, stature and transverse chest diameter. The ratio stature/transverse-chest-diameter provides an index of the body build which is free from the influence of general body size. On this measure the XYY patients were mesomorphic (suggesting that as well as being tall, their overall build is proportionate to this). The matched control group came out as endomorphic.

The recent physical examinations of the 26 patients currently in Rampton who have chromosomal abnormalities revealed that the arm span was greater than the height in 10 of the 13 XYY patients, in 6 of the 9 XXY group and in none of the 4 XXYY group. Thus, the span/height difference does not differ significantly from normal as the span is greater than the height in the normal male and in patients with Klinefelter's syndrome (Stewart *et al.*, 1959).

Frontal baldness, talipes, goitre and the special syndromes (all of which features are reported in the literature as being found in association with chromosomal abnormalities) were not present in any of the 26 patients, although 1 patient, an XYY, had had an angioma of the left temporal lobe removed at the age of 10 years. None of the patients were considered to

TABLE 5

Physical examination (*b*)

	XYY (N=13)	XXY (N=9)	XXYY (N=4)
Sexual			
Hypogonadism	1	9	4
Small penis	–	6	1
Scanty or absent body hair	–	4	–
Scanty or absent facial hair	0	1	4
Neurological			
Epilepsy	2	4	–
Intention tremor	2	1	3
Other neurological abnormality	5	4	1

have congenital hypotonia; delayed osseous development was thought to be too difficult to assess reliably. Only 1 patient had a cataract which had developed later in life. There were no congenital opacities (a condition found fairly frequently in patients with chromosomal abnormality). Some degree of high arched palate was found in many of the patients but this is a common finding in patients of any comparable subnormality group.

Urinary testosterone excretion rates were measured in 15 patients detained at Rampton. Of these, 9 had an XYY chromosome complement and the remaining 6 had a normal male sex chromosome pattern. Almost all these patients had higher excretory rates of testosterone compared to normal healthy men (Rudd *et al.*, 1968) but this is almost certainly an effect of institutionalisation.

XXY patients

All members of this group had a marked degree of hypogonadism, the size of the penis was small in 6 of the 9 patients and 1 had an absent right testicle. Abnormality in the quantity of body hair found in these subjects was hard to assess as there is great variation in normals; however, it was noted as absent in 1, scanty in 3 and excessive in 1. Facial hair was normal in 8 and poor in 1. Pubic hair was normal in distribution in all but one case. Four of these patients were epileptics (25%) as compared with a figure of 20.4% for epilepsy in the total male population. Other neurological abnormalities found were hypotonia of the upper limbs with an unsteadiness of gait in 1 patient, weakness in 1 limb in 2 patients and bilateral ptosis in 1 patient. There was one case with dysdiadochokinesis, who also presented asymmetry of the face.

XYY patients

Apart from the tendency to increased stature (Court Brown, 1968), there was no special characteristic of the XYY group. One showed marked asymmetry of the face and another unilateral gynaecomastia; but no definite asymmetry could be found in any other parts of the body amongst this group. The quantity of body hair found was normal as also was facial hair; pubic hair distribution was normal. One patient, however, showed hypogonadism and a further 2 a degree of softness of the testes. In all members of this group, the size of the penis was normal.

Two of the 13 patients had epilepsy (15.3%). Intention tremor (mentioned by Daly, 1969b, as being commonly found in patients with an XYY constitution) was only found in 2 patients. Several, however, showed unco-ordination in the lower limbs in the heel-knee test; 2 had brisk jaw jerks, 1 showed dysdiadochokinesis in one arm, 1 had hypotonia in the upper limbs and 1 had some unsteadiness and weakness of both legs which may have been accentuated by head injury. In all, 5 of the XYY patients showed some neurological abnormality.

Psychological examination

The results of psychological investigations are summarised in Table 6. The XYY patients tended to be slightly more intelligent than the controls, the Klinefelter's less intelligent; but the difference is small and not statistically significant. In Little's study, out of 46 psychological variables in the test administered, only 2 showed any significant difference between the means of the XYY group and the matched controls. These were:-

Factor O of the I.P.A.T. 16 personality factor inventory. The controls scored themselves as more worrying and anxious, easily upset, hypochondriacal, lonely and brooding.

Endurance (on the Edwards Personal Preference Schedule). The controls tended to score themselves as having less persistence at jobs of work or problems and as being more easily distracted than the XYY group.

There were no differences in neuroticism, extraversion and lying in a test situation as measured by the Eysenck Personality Inventory. Little concluded that from the results of these studies, there seemed to be few real differences between XYY and non-XYY patients at Rampton. He considered that the measures used might have revealed characteristics common to the "Rampton patients" rather than to any specific group. This

TABLE 6

Psychological characteristics

	XYY	Controls	XXY
I.Q. (mean)	81.6	74.9	72.7
I.P.A.T. Factor O	low	high*	N.K.
E.P.P.S. "Endurance"	high	low*	N.K.
G.S.R.	N.K.		lower conditioning*

* significant at < .05

was thought not altogether surprising since there are various social pressures in an institution like Rampton to which all the patients are subjected which will affect responses on personality measures.

McKerracher (1968) compared a group of XXY patients with a similar number of matched controls and found a lower level of G.S.R. reactivity during a classical conditioning procedure in the XXY group. He also found a WAIS performance bias more often in this group.

Behaviour in Rampton

The behaviour of both the XYY and XXY patients tended to be better than that of the controls whilst in hospital.

TABLE 7

Behaviour in Rampton

	XYY (N=22)	Controls (N=50)	XXY (N=16)
Aggressive behaviour			
against property	3 (11%)	7 (14%)	3 (17%)
against staff	2 (9%)	13 (26%)	2 (11%)
against patients	8 (37%)	28 (56%)	5 (28%)
Good relationships with staff	20 (90%)**	27 (54%)	13 (81%)
Homosexual liaisons with other patients	2 (9%)**	19 (38%)	0 (0)
Medication (psychotropic)	3 (15%)	16 (32%)	4 (22%)

** significant at < .01

There is a significant difference in the type of relationship reported by the staff as far as the patients with chromosomal abnormality are concerned, in both instances being more favourable. These patients were also less likely to form homosexual relationships with other patients. This trend towards better behaviour is, perhaps, also indicated by the fact that there was less need for psychotropic drugs to be given to these patients. However, it must be remembered that some of the controls (and none of the other 2 groups) were classified as suffering from a mental illness.

Again, this trend for the XXY's and XYY's to get on better in hospital is shown by the relative length of time which they spend in hospital as a whole, as well as by the length of time spent in the more secure part of it.

TABLE 8

Length of stay and re-admission rate

	XYY (N=22)	Controls (N=50)	XXY (N=16)
Length of stay in Rampton	6.7 years	8.2 years	6.9 years
Length of stay in blocks	4.8 years	6.0 years	4.3 years
Re-admission rate	4 (18%)	10 (20%)	4 (22%)

Hospital instability, as indicated by failure in the Villa Wards and return to the Block Wards, occurred in 7% of XYY's, 14% of the controls and 11% of the XXY's. The difference is not statistically significant but is in the same direction as the other findings. There was no significant difference in re-admission rates.

Discussion

The number of patients with chromosomal abnormality is very small when they are broken down into their respective groups, and it is not surprising that one can indicate only trends in behaviour patterns. Among the findings shown in this paper, it is of interest that significantly more of the XYY patients were classified as suffering from psychopathic disorder. (It should be stressed that the classification 'Psychopathic Disorder' is used here in its legal sense.) This may, in part, be a reflection of the fact that more of those with chromosome abnormalities are coming from the courts. The fact that the XYY patients tend to be of slightly higher I.Q. may also contribute to this difference.

There does seem to be a high incidence of neurological disorder in these patients and it is hoped at a later date to make some further assessment of this within other groups in hospital.

Although few differences in personality factors distinguish those with chromosomal abnormality from the rest of the Rampton population, there does seem to be some real difference in behaviour that these patients show at Rampton. On the basis of the present information, it is not possible to assess exactly what characteristics determine this while yet failing to assist them in a better adjustment to the outside world than the controls. The follow-up information, however, is at present still very sparse and it may be that some other factors may be discovered later.

Acknowledgments

We should like to thank the Special Hospitals Research Unit for their help and advice, and also the Department of Human Genetics at Sheffield University.

E.E.G. FINDINGS IN MALE PATIENTS WITH SEX CHROMOSOME
ABNORMALITIES IN A SECURITY PRISON

Elman W. Poole

Introduction

H.M. Prison Grendon is a special security prison for the psychiatric investigation and treatment of offenders. Its Neurophysiological Department has been able to carry out routine E.E.G. tests on almost all receptions since 1965; the aim has been to provide not only the usual diagnostic facilities but also to obtain neurophysiological data to be used along with other findings (e.g. clinical, psychological, criminal) in the hope of categorizing different classes of disorder. Though E.E.G. work has been limited by staff and equipment problems, it has included quantifying and research procedures; and the department has had the advantage of being developed in conjunction with Oxford General Hospital Services which have provided comparative figures (as well as special training and assistance). Most of the accumulated results still await definitive analysis, and this paper concerns those aspects relevant to genetic abnormalities which have been studied by the Oxford M.R.C. Population Genetics Research Unit in their two surveys. The first, which was carried out in 1967-8 on 204 subjects by Dr. Bartlett, has already been published (Bartlett *et al.*, 1968). This work was resumed again in February 1969, and this second survey continues (over 132 inmates examined).

Material and Methods

Grendon Population

Grendon admits approximately 250 patients per year and averages about 180-200 inmates (all male) who are usually referred for psychiatric investigation and/or treatment, but are not "certifiable", or suffering from appreciable intellectual impairment or permanent organic cerebral changes. In the majority of cases the diagnosis is psychopathic, and the distribution of personality traits has been found to be approximately 45% for antisocial, immature and inadequate traits, and 25% for sexual deviancy. Principal psychiatric traits or symptoms have been assessed as psychopathic (80%), neurotic (60%), anxiety and depression (40-50%).

The ages range from 16-65 years, with a mean of 26.9 years and s.d. of 8.7 (one sample of 340). For E.E.G. purposes it has been found convenient to have 3 age groupings.

        a) **Young** 16-20 yrs (25% approximately);
        b) **Middle** 21-31 yrs (50% approximately);
        c) **Old**   32-   yrs (25% approximately).

Criminal records for the present offence leading to admission to Grendon show 70% crimes against property, and 30% crimes against the person (sex in half). Arson is the current offence in 5-6%. The average number of previous convictions is about 8.

The intelligence level of inmates is seldom low and the Ravens progressive matrices average score has been found to be approximately 41.7 (±7.8 s.d.). Details of psychometric tests carried out routinely are not included here.

The characteristics of the population are important because, with this continuing genetic survey, it has not been considered worthwhile to provide precisely matched comparative data until the survey has been closed, and thus the general Grendon population characteristics have been used for comparison.

E.E.G. Studies

With stick-on Ag-AgCl electrodes (10/20 system), 16-channel waking records with overbreathing and photic stimulation have been carried out routinely on an Offner TC machine and have included frequency analysis by means of a 2-channel B.N.I. waveform analyser. In a limited number, sleep records (natural or seconal-induced) have also been obtained. In one series of successive receptions ("R" set; n=340) an analysis of frequency content of limb tremor was also included as described previously (Poole *et al.*, 1966). In a further series ("B" set; n=330) this was omitted. Records have been assessed independently of other relevant variables (e.g. genetic in this instance) and kept in a form readily permitting independent reappraisal. In addition to arbitrary overall grading of abnormality (0 normal; + normal-slight; ++ slight; +++ slight-moderate; ++++ moderate; +++++ moderate-severe), the frequency content of the record has been assessed from the analyser abundance write-outs for four 10-second epochs and several features extracted, as described previously (Poole *et al.*, 1966; Poole & Taylor, 1970), e.g.

1. Mean (centre of gravity) frequency in 3-16 cps range
2. Dominant frequency in 6-12 cps range (or 8-13 cps)
3. Dominant frequency in 3-7 cps range
4. Minimum frequency in 2-7 cps range

In the "R" set this has been for P_3O_1 derivation with eyes closed (arm elevated, and arm resting) and associated with tremor analysis. In the second "B" set this has been for C_3P_3, in the resting eyes-closed state. Other derivations (e.g. temporal) are available for measuring.

Genetically abnormal cases had all been examined routinely and assessed before the abnormality was detected; but they were then usually re-examined (including sleep records) to check the consistency of findings and to obtain data precisely comparable with the "R" set. On the 12 genetically abnormal cases, 21 records were taken including 9 sleep studies (9 patients).

Comparative/Control Groups

Precise matching of genetically abnormal cases with those from prison and other sources has not been attempted since the survey is continuing.

1. Records from a small group of 12 genetically normal inmates, matched for age and usually over 180 cms tall were mixed with those from the 12 genetically abnormal subjects and reported on 'blind' by a skilled observer. The groups were then reviewed with the author in relation to his previous routine reports, with good agreement. These "matched" controls would be extended when the survey closed.

2. Results from a control group of 38 inmates used in the previous study (Bartlett *et al.*, 1968) were no longer precisely comparable but have been noted.

3. Results from the main Grendon "R" group (340 inmates) have been indicated where relevant, since these represent the general Grendon population against which the results are judged, though not age-matched.

4. Results from general hospital patients (n=378) and normal subjects (n=109) at the Churchill Hospital, Oxford, have also been noted, but age and sex differences prevent fine distinctions from being drawn; and even though the examination techniques were identical, instrumental

differences cannot be excluded. The age sub-groupings were not the same as for Grendon inmates.

Drug therapy and night sedatives are important since these may influence E.E.G. findings and frequency content; and it is difficult to allow for this, especially in retrospective studies. Grendon patients "on drugs" i.e. receiving such medication within 1 week of an E.E.G. have slightly lower dominant and mean frequency E.E.G. values than other inmates, but not in all age groups; tremor values appear less consistently different. One of the genetically abnormal patients was receiving a tranquillizer, and 4 others may have had a small regular night barbiturate sedative. Two of the 12 control subjects were receiving a tranquillizer or barbiturate. It seemed unlikely that these drugs disturbed the essential findings and group differences to an important extent, but a larger series would be needed for this to be taken into account.

Results*

General Findings

An outline of physical, criminal, and psychological features appears in Table 1 (where available) for the 12 cases, listed in age order - 5 XYY and then 7 XXY (including 1 mosaic XY/XXY). An above-average height is present in 9 cases (all the XXY's). Head injury of at least minor degree was reported in 4 patients. In one patient (G6) probable epileptic attacks were reported but were not a current problem and there seemed to have been no anticonvulsant therapy. The age of first conviction is average or subaverage in 7 patients; and the ratio of crimes against property/person is low at 1/1. (Grendon average 7/3, but in the 12 matched controls 7/5). The number of previous convictions tends to be below average (in 8 patients). Arson appears in the present conviction offence in two patients (Grendon average 5%); it appears in previous offences of 4 other patients and indeed all the XYY's had arson in their criminal record (Grendon average approx. 7%, or estimated 5% if genetically abnormal were excluded). The Raven matrices scores are scattered above and below the usual Grendon score, and in no case is the level particularly low, nor are there any clear group differences.

E.E.G. Findings

In Table 2 appear E.E.G. and limb tremor data, again first for the 5 XYY and then the 7 XXY groups, in age order. The overall abnormality '+' grade shows a greater abnormality in the genetic abnormal groups than in any "control" group, with emphasis on the XXY. In the genetic groups 7/12 had at least moderate abnormality (Figs. 1 and 2), which was present in only 1/12 of the matched controls and in 10-15% of the Grendon population. None of the genetic cases was considered normal, whereas 4/12 of controls had little or no abnormality. However, the alpha-frequency range and dominant frequency was rather slow (<9cps) in only 4 instances (3 XXY; 1 XYY), but improved on another occasion. The mean frequency was subaverage in 8 instances (3/5 XYY; 5/7 XXY), reflecting the increased slow wave content. It might be noted that peak alpha amplitudes were frequently higher in the genetic abnormal group. The abnormalities appeared largely as added slow components tending to be maximal temporally and frontally and accentuated slight-moderate on overbreathing. This slow activity occurred at times in bursts and there were ill-defined sharp elements which occurred more especially in the XXY's (Fig. 2). With photic stimulation, abnormality (or uncertainty) was confined to the XYY group (5/6 cases); and such findings are uncommon in Grendon material (Figs. 2 and 3).

* Notes on 2 additional cases appear in the addendum.

In sleep records abnormalities were not very distinctive. Occasional sharp elements occurred in most cases without particular group differences. Search for 14 and 6/sec positive spikes was not rewarding (as is common in Grendon and Oxford Departments despite the routine use of ear reference montages). Comparison with Grendon material is difficult in that only select cases have sleep traces at present.

As already indicated much the same type of E.E.G. disturbance occurs in a minority of Grendon patients, presumably without sex chromosomal abnormality though further genetic study (e.g. of the relative size of the Y chromosome) may possibly reveal more subtle types of anomaly. The E.E.G. appearances are illustrated in Fig. 3 from two XY patients; both showed moderate abnormalities and in one (Fig. 3B) these were provoked by photic stimulation, though there was no history of convulsive disorder.

Tremor Findings

Mean (3-16 cps) and dominant (6-12 cps) frequency values appeared rather low in the genetically abnormal groups. In 7-8/12 patients the mean was subaverage; but in 10/12 the dominant was subaverage (4 cases >2 s.d.'s down), whereas a subaverage dominant occurred in only 2 of the 12 controls.

Frequency Analysis Features: Genetic Abnormality

With regard to the frequency values such as mean, dominant (6-12 cps), dominant (3-7 cps), and minimum (2-7 cps), it is of interest to see whether any particular values carried a higher "risk" of genetic abnormality.

The mean (centre of gravity) values for E.E.G. and tremor are illustrated in Fig. 4. The normalized population distributions are shown for Grendon inmates (D), and above for 3 groups examined similarly at the Churchill Hospital (A, normals; B, patients with nil/slight E.E.G. abnormality; and C, patients with moderate or greater abnormality). The individual abnormal genetic cases are entered along the bottom at their respective E.E.G. and tremor values. There are progressive shifts to the slow end as the E.E.G. disturbance increases, and Grendon inmates fall between the two patient groups (B and C). The genetic cases are scattered but show a slight tendency to fall towards the lower part of the prison distribution; they form, however, a considerable contrast with the normal groups (A) though the comparison is not necessarily valid. The corresponding analyses of tremor mean results show more scatter in all groups, but the differences between groups are not so distinct, and the genetic cases are only minimally biased towards the lower end of the prison population. Since the technical and sampling problems would be much the same for both E.E.G. and tremor analyses such a dual comparison is particularly relevant.

Other E.E.G. frequency values have been analysed and displayed in the same way in Fig. 5 as population distributions for comparison. The data have come from the same Normal (A), Oxford Hospital (B and C), and Grendon (D) groups, and three aspects have been considered - 2-7 cps minimum, 3-7 cps dominant, 6-12 cps dominant abundance. The individual genetic case values have been entered below. Grendon patients resemble most the Oxford (B) normal-slight group. The genetically abnormal cases appear to have a rather low minimum (2-7 cps), and a high dominant (3-7 cps) and possibly a low dominant in the 6-12 cps range; but the clustering is not very distinctive. The corresponding analyses for tremor appear in Fig. 6 and the same general observations can be made, though the populations show more scatter and there is a clearer predominance of lower values in the 6-12 cps range.

A larger series of genetically abnormal cases would make such comparisons more worthwhile. There appears to be no striking concentration of genetic abnormality in any one section of these E.E.G. or tremor populations (except possibly in the 3-7 cps dominant), and indeed this would not be expected from the type of disturbance observed in the raw E.E.G.

Height/E.E.G. Abnormality/Genetic Abnormality

It is worth considering whether, by taking account of overall E.E.G. abnormality, and height, and some of these frequency characteristics, a useful discriminant function for genetic abnormality might be obtained. This also permits critical examination of the tall prisoners. One approach is illustrated in Fig. 7A and 7B where, for the 25% of patients whose height is 180 cms or over, height has been plotted against dominant frequency (6-12 cps) in (A) and mean frequency (3-16 cps) in (B). The cases have been coded according to E.E.G. abnormality with an indication as to whether they have been checked genetically:

(O, less than moderate E.E.G. abnormality; if XY checked Δ)
(●, at least moderate E.E.G. abnormality; if XY checked ▲)

The abnormal genetic cases (x+) are in fact still too sparse (five* only) to provide any indication as to areas of particular suspicion. The incidence of E.E.G. abnormality is rather high but there is little clustering and no particular involvement of the very tall, though there may be something unusual in the height distribution towards the upper half. Computer discriminant analysis along the lines of Batchelor's work would seem indicated.† It is noteworthy that genetic screening using height (180 cms and above) as a criterion and examining the top 25% of subjects would have detected only about half the abnormal cases.

E.E.G. Features, Intelligence and Height

Some brief points on these aspects are worth including despite the small series. In the genetically abnormal patients there seems to be a relationship between E.E.G. abnormality ('+' grading) and I.Q., the more abnormal having the lower scores (r=-0.5). This can also be seen in frequency content, the lower values occurring with the lower intelligence scores (e.g. for E.E.G. mean, r = +0.4). A correlation of this type has been found in some other Grendon groups, at a statistically significant level (unlike these).

There may also be a correlation between E.E.G. content and height, and this has been found to a limited extent in other Grendon groups but needs further study. There is little evidence to suggest any association between I.Q. and height, though this has not yet been studied specially at Grendon. The possibility that height might predispose to head trauma, brain damage and criminality is not strongly supported.

Conclusion

In this particular prison population, E.E.G. abnormalities appear to be associated with genetic defects without mental intellectual impairment or overt epilepsy. There are probably significant differences between XXY and XYY groups; the Klinefelter is the more suspect for paroxysmal tendency, in keeping with a previous report by Hambert and Frey (1964), though the preponderance of slow dominant alpha rhythms in their patients is not well confirmed in this study. The abnormalities do not seem

* Seven including 2 from addendum.
† Batchelor, B.G. and Wilkins, B.R. *Adaptive discriminant functions.* I.E.E. Conference Publ., no. 42, 1968.

exceptional or particularly distinctive, and occur at lower incidence in
the rest of Grendon cases without obvious cause. However, detailed
studies are needed to assess such aspects and to see if the genetically
normal and abnormal individuals with distinct E.E.G. disturbance have
anything more in common than the disturbed E.E.G. It would seem of
interest to consider the relative amount of Y chromosome material in
relation to E.E.G. as well as to other features, and the work of
Nielsen (1968b) using the Y/F ratio would seem a particularly promising
approach to a combined genetic multi-disciplinary study for computer
analysis. Unfortunately such assessments of the Y chromosome have not
been available at Grendon so far.

It is not yet possible in Grendon material to provide any reasonable
E.E.G.-plus-physical features which would arouse suspicion as to genetic
constitution (though a tall, dull, patient with an abnormal E.E.G. and
photosensitivity would seem a promising start). Detailed analysis of
general Grendon material (clinical, criminal, psychometric, E.E.G., etc.)
may well clarify the significance of E.E.G. disturbances in behavioural
terms, and suggest their contribution, if any, to the production of an
habitual/unsuccessful way of criminal life.

Summary

At a security prison* for the psychiatric treatment of offenders
(particularly those with psychopathy), E.E.G. studies have been carried
out routinely since 1965 on over 800 male patients as part of a multi-
disciplinary study of prisoners. In two chromosomal surveys (one of 205
inmates, and another, still proceeding, of over 132 inmates) undertaken
by the Medical Research Council Population Genetics Research Unit, Oxford,
12 individuals of abnormal karyotype have so far been identified. E.E.G.
and other electrophysiological data from these subjects have been compared
according to karyotype (5 XYY, 7 XXY or mosaic) and contrasted with
prison control groups and with the general prison findings. Observations
on psychiatric history, criminal record and psychological features are
briefly noted, and include a high incidence of arson and above-average
height. E.E.G. abnormalities appear greater in the genetically abnormal
groups with emphasis on the XXY karyotype in which photic responses tend
to be unusual, but disturbances are not specially increased in sleep.
E.E.G. features appear related to intelligence but not clearly to height.
The possibility of predicting the most genetically suspect individuals
from E.E.G. and other physical features is discussed. It would seem of
interest to relate E.E.G. findings to the relative size of the Y chromosome in XY individuals.

Addendum

Two further cases, kindly provided from non-Grendon sources, have been
examined and also show E.E.G. abnormality and unusual height; data have
been entered in the figures where possible and are as follows:

1. XYY: aged $17\frac{1}{2}$ yrs, height 199.5 cms. Father was mentally disturbed and
epileptic, brother had renal disease and patient had ? congenital
bladder abnormality. Had committed acts of wanton damage,
threatened bodily violence, and made suicidal gestures. Present
conviction concerned possession of an offensive weapon. I.Q. 88
(Matrices 34).
E.E.G.: moderate abnormality; 9-10 cps alpha activity and an excess of
intermediate slow components tending to occur in bursts and to be sharply
contoured; no special features in sleep.
Frequency content (cps):- E.E.G. 6-12 dominant = 9; mean = 8.6; Tremor

* H.M. Prison Grendon, Grendon Underwood, Aylesbury, Bucks.

6-12 dominant = 10; mean = 8.2
E.E.G. records 18 months and 12 months previously were also abnormal.

2. XXY: aged 28 yrs, height 183.5 cms. Family history, nothing special
   known. Non-identical twin (? epileptic). Appendicitis and
   peritonitis aged 17. Aggressive and destructive behaviour; on
   probation at 16 yr; strangling gestures towards girls, and one more
   serious attempt. In mental hospitals, diagnosed ? schizophrenia,
   treatment including E.C.T. aged 21. Possible amnesic episodes.
   I.Q. Matrices 117; Wechsler full scale 98.
E.E.G.: moderate abnormality; 8-9 cps alpha activity and a bilateral excess
of mixed intermediate-slow and slow components maximal temporally (posterior) and at times sharp; limited subharmonics and sharp waves with photic
stimulation; a few sharp and slow wave bursts in sleep.
Frequency content (cps):- E.E.G. 6-12 dominant = 8; mean = 9.0; Tremor 6-12
dominant = 8, mean = 8.2.
E.E.G. records 3 and 4 years previously were also abnormal. Patient on
drug therapy.

Acknowledgements

The encouragement and assistance of Dr. Gray, Medical Superintendent,
H.M. Prison Grendon, and Staff has been invaluable in this collaborative
project undertaken in conjunction with the Oxford M.R.C. Population
Genetics Research Unit with Dr. Stevenson, Dr. Bartlett and Mrs. Unrau.
The studies owe much to enthusiastic efforts of Hospital Officers I. Booth
and M. Storm, and to Mrs. J. Chartres and Miss M. Beauchamp of Churchill
Hospital, Oxford.

TABLE 1: CLINICAL AND CRIMINAL RECORD DATA IN 12 MALES OF ABNORMAL KARYOTYPE

	Age (yrs)	Ht. (cms)	Wt. (kg.)	Medical history	Psychiatric diagnosis (International classification)	Age at first conviction	Convictions: Number and type of previous offences	Present Offence(s)	Non-verbal intelligence Ravens matrices (I.Q. approx.)
XXY									
G1	19	174.0	66.5	Minor head injury, suicidal attempts	Not available	8	9 blackmail, arson x 2, dishonesty.	Demanding money with menaces.	34 (85)
G2	19	175.3	62.1	Head injury 1967 and 1968; left-handed.	Not available	13	10 dishonesty, indecent exposure, cars, arson.	Dishonesty, Car offences	55 (125)
G3	22	177.8	70.1		1. Schizoid personality 2. Sexual deviation - homosexuality 3. Drug addiction (amphetamines)	17	6 arson, larceny, fraud, sacrilege.	Taking and driving away car.	46 (105)
G4	34	182.9	66.1	Dizzy spells years age.	1. Schizoid personality 2. Anxiety reaction 3. Sexual deviation - homosexuality	34	1st offence	Threatened suicide, arson for revenge.	33 (90)
G5	45	196.9	85.7	R.T.A. (? Right parietal)	Not available	22	20 dishonesty and arson.	Robbery with violence.	44 (115)
XXY KLINEFELTER									
G6	21	203.2	114.7	Sister diabetic. ? Hypothyroid on thyroxine since 11 years.	Not available	19	6 dishonesty - cars.	Dishonesty - cars.	38 (90)

	Age (yrs)	Ht. (cms)	Wt. (kg.)	Medical history	Psychiatric diagnosis (International classification)	Age at first conviction	Convictions: Number and type of previous offences	Present Offence(s)	Non-verbal intelligence Ravens matrices (I.Q. approx.)
XXY KLINEFELTER (cont.)									
G7	24	181.6	60.2	Head injuries, right temporal scar.	1. Immature personality	17	3 car offences, malicious damage.	Arson for excitement.	49 (110)
G8	29	177.8	73.5	Twin (also psychiatric patient) was left-handed.	Not available	22	4 all dishonesty.	Robbery with violence, assault-G.B.H.	39 (95)
G9	29	182.9	70.3	Nephrectomy 1968 and other operations.	1. Personality disorder	28	1st offence	Indecent assault, gross indecency.	53 (120)
G10	33	179.1	63.5	Many suicide attempts, ambidextrous.	Not available	30	2 violence, drunk and disorderly.	Malicious wounding, larceny.	30 (85)
G11	37	179.1	57.0	? Head injury as child.	Not available	19	4 burglary, larceny, violence, rape.	Burglary and sex-attack on elderly female.	28 (88)
XY/XXY/MOSAIC									
G12	36	172.7	87.8		1. Inadequate personality. 2. Sexual deviation – polymorphous	17	10 burglary, larceny, indecent assault.	Burglary with motivation.	45 (112)
Previous[1] Controls n = 38	22–36	175.3 ± 6.1	96.2 ±6.6				7 ± 4.5		41.3 ± 6.8
General Grendon Population n = 340	26.9 ±8.7	175.5 ± 7.2			>70% Psychopathic (aggressive inadequate)	19	8	Arson 5½%	41.7 ± 7.8

Reference: [1] Bartlett et. al., 1968.

TABLE 2: E.E.G. AND LIMB TREMOR DATA FOR 12 MALES OF ABNORMAL KARYOTYPE

	Age (yrs)	Overall abnormality grade	Waking-resting E.E.G. record			Hyper-ventilation slow wave increase	Photic stimulation	Sleep record features	Finger tremor frequencies	
			Frequency Content Alpha Activity dom. range cps	Mean 3-16 cps 8-13+ cps or 6-12φ P30₁	Abnormalities of θ and Δ / Sharp wave activity				Mean 3-16 cps	Dom. 6-12 cps
XYY										
G1	19	++++	9-10	10 / 8.3	Widespread mixed maximal temporally + bursts (R>L) / /	Moderate	F (R>L)	Occasional sharp and slow waves bilaterally	8.0	9.0
G2	19	+++	9½-10	9 / 9.3	Rhythmic θ frontally + ragged mixed bursts / /	Slight-moderate ragged bursts frontally/temporally	F H	Anterior slow/sharp bursts. Unusual recurring features. Few positive spikes.	9.6	11.0
G3	22	+++	9-10	9 / 8.1	Slight/moderate θ maximal temporally / Few ant. temporal L>R	Slight	F	No record	6.7	6.0
G4	34	++++	8-9	8 / 7.8	Widespread mixed frequency runs maximal post-central + bursts / /	Moderate R>L	F S	Slow increased with sharp waves. Asymmetries.	8.8	8.0
G5	45	++	9-10½	10 / 9.2	Occasional runs centrally + bursts anteriorly / Few pre-centrally	Slight	F (R>L)	Unusual mixed recurring slow/fast/sharp waves bilaterally. Some positive.	9.1	7.0
XXY										
G6	21	++++	7½-9½	8 / 7.5	Widespread θ maximal anteriorly + Δ bursts. / /	Moderate	F H S	Sharp fast frontally	7.9	9.0

	Age (yrs)	Overall abnormality grade	Waking-resting E.E.G. record: Frequency Content: Alpha range cps	Activity dom. cps 8-13† or 6-12ϕ	Mean 3-16 cps P_3O_1	Abnormalities of θ and Δ	Sharp wave activity	Hyperventilation slow wave increase	Photic stimulation	Sleep record features	Finger tremor frequencies: Mean 3-16 cps	Dom. 6-12 cps
XXY (cont.)												
G7	24	*++++	10-12	11	8.8	Anterior runs mainly θ + few widespread Δ waves	Few maximal temporally	Moderate sharp waves L>R	F (L>R) ?unrelated slow wave complexes	Anterior slow runs increased with few sharp waves.	7.2	6.0
G8	29	++++	9-10	10	9.2	Mixed θ + runs maximal anterior temporally	Few L>R	Slight L>R	F (R>L) Slow increased ? sensitivity	No record	8.4	9.0
G9	29	*+++	8-9½	8	8.4	Widespread mixed runs/bursts anteriorly	Few anteriorly	Slight	F H ?unrelated bursts	Anterior slow runs/bursts R>L	9.4	11.0
G10	33	++++	7-9	8	8.1	Runs maximal fronto/temporally (L>R) + sharp bursts	Sharp θ	Moderate	F H Unsustained slow/sharp waves	Anterior runs + sharp waves increased. Mixed bursts/sharp waves	8.3	7.0
G11	37	+++++	9½-11	10	8.3	Runs/bursts anteriorly and posteriorly L>R, sharp θ	Sharp θ	Slight (L>R)	F H Unsustained sharp/slow	No record	9.3	9.0
XY/XXY												
G12	36	++	8½-10	9	7.8	Scattered θ and Δ postcentrally	/	Slight	F (L>R)	Slight asymmetries	8.5	8.0

	Age (yrs)	Overall abnormality grade	Waking-resting E.E.G. record							Finger tremor frequencies	
			Frequency Content Alpha Activity range dom. cps 8-13† cps or 6-12φ	Mean 3-16 cps P30l	Abnormalities of θ and Δ	Sharp wave activity	Hyperventilation slow wave increase	Photic stimulation	Sleep record features	Mean 3-16 cps	Dom. 6-12 cps
Previous[1] controls mean n = 38	...	...	10.0 ±.75	9.0 ±.68	Approx. 10-15% have moderate or greater abnormality	...	...	...	...	8.9 ±.72	9.5 ±1.6
General Grendon population n = 340 Mean and s.d.	...	++ - +++	9.6† 9.5φ ±0.93	8.8 ±0.74	Approx. 10-15% have moderate or greater abnormality	...	...	...	...	8.7 ±0.84	9.9 ±1.43
Matched tall controls Mean n = 12	...	++	9.0φ ±0.57	8.7 ±0.14	1/12 Moderate abnormality	...	...	1/12 subh.	...	8.9 ±.4	10.0 ±1.1

Reference: [1] Bartlett et al., 1968

† 8-13 cps range
φ 6-12 cps range

F = Fundamental following.
H = harmonic following.
S = Subharmonic following.

* Less abnormality on another record.

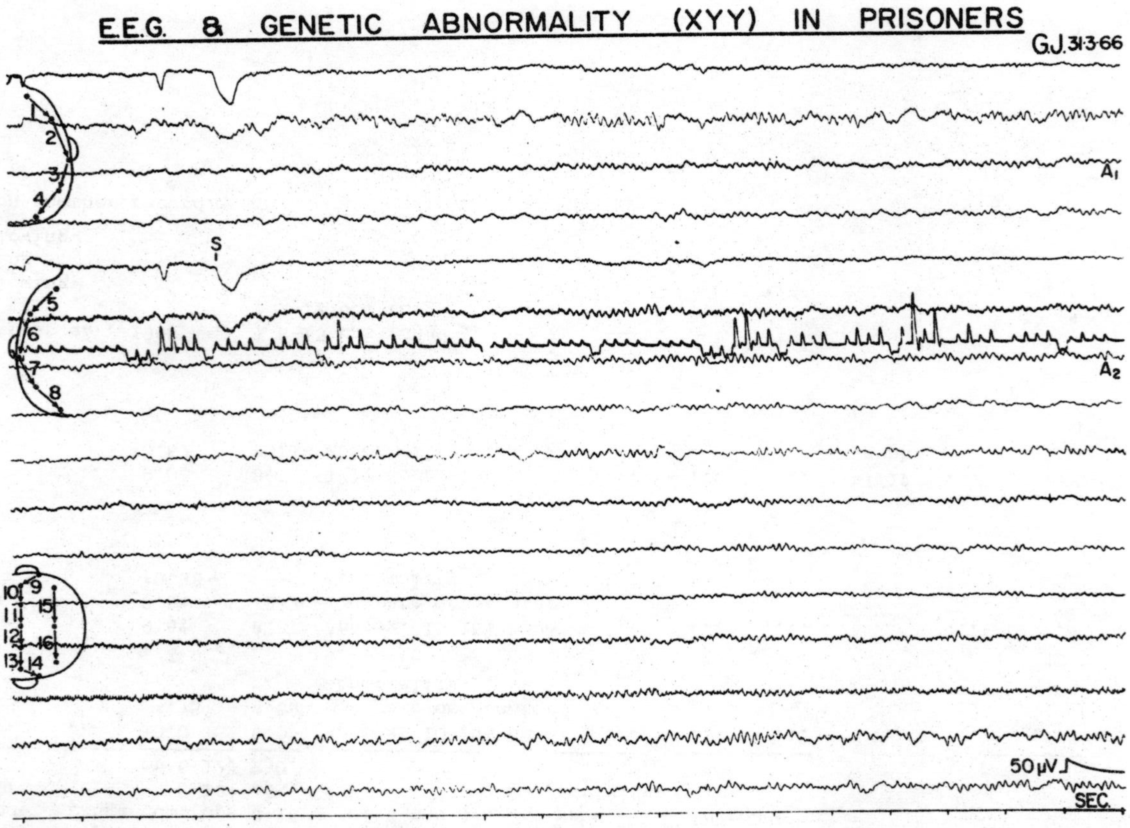

E.E.G. 8 GENETIC ABNORMALITY (XYY) IN PRISONERS

GJ.3┽3·66

A₁

A₂

S

50µV

SEC.

Fig. 1. E.E.G. abnormality in an XYY inmate (G4) aged 34; first offence, arson for revenge and suicide attempt; I.Q. 90. E.E.G. shows moderate abnormality; alpha activity is at 8-9 cps and there is a widespread excess of slow components maximal in temporal areas with right emphasis. (S indicates eye closure in this and subsequent figures.)

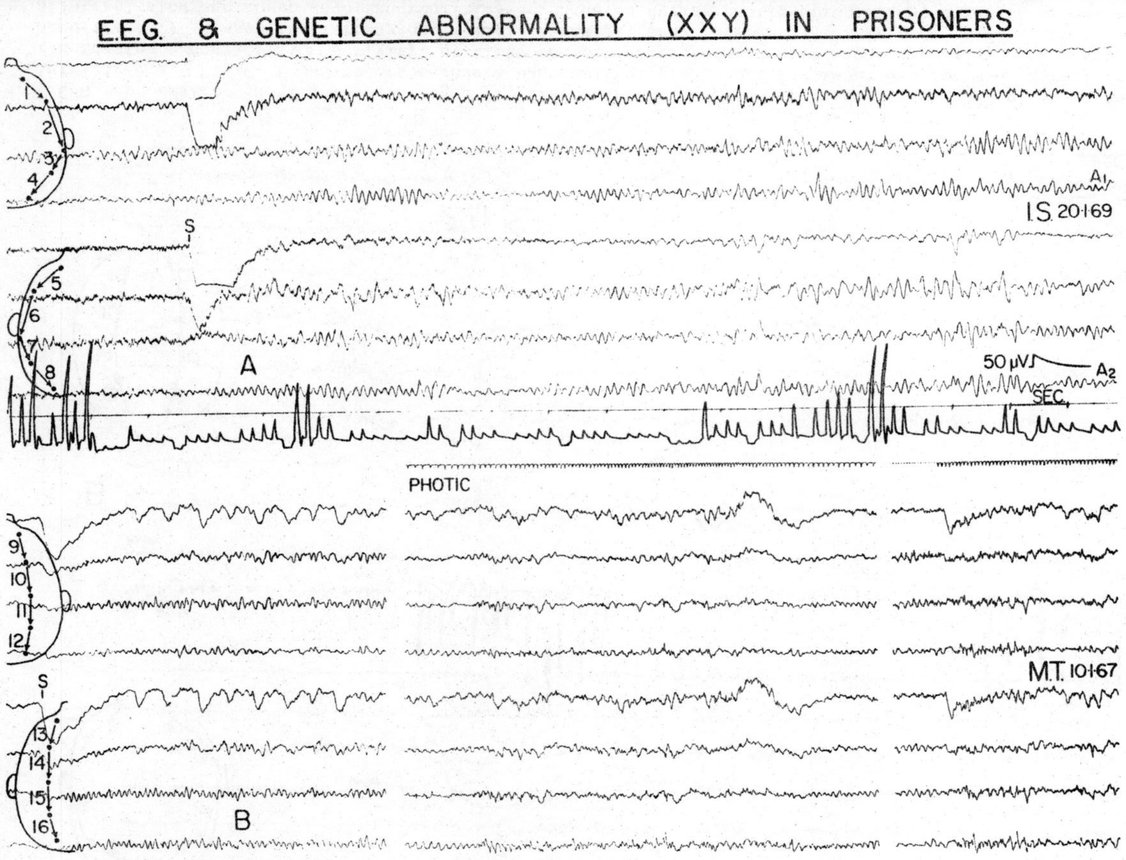

Fig. 2. E.E.G. abnormality in XXY inmates. <u>A</u> aged 33 (G10); malicious wounding, larceny and suicidal attempts; I.Q. 85. E.E.G. shows moderate abnormality; alpha activity is at 7-9cps, and there are widespread runs of mixed frequency slow activity, at times sharply contoured and with left emphasis. (Analyser write-out hand-traced.) <u>B</u> aged 37 (G11); burglary and attempted rape of an old woman; I.Q. 88. E.E.G. shows moderate abnormality; alpha activity is at 10-11cps, and photic stimulation is associated with unsustained sharp and slow waves; runs of mixed slow activity appeared in the resting record.

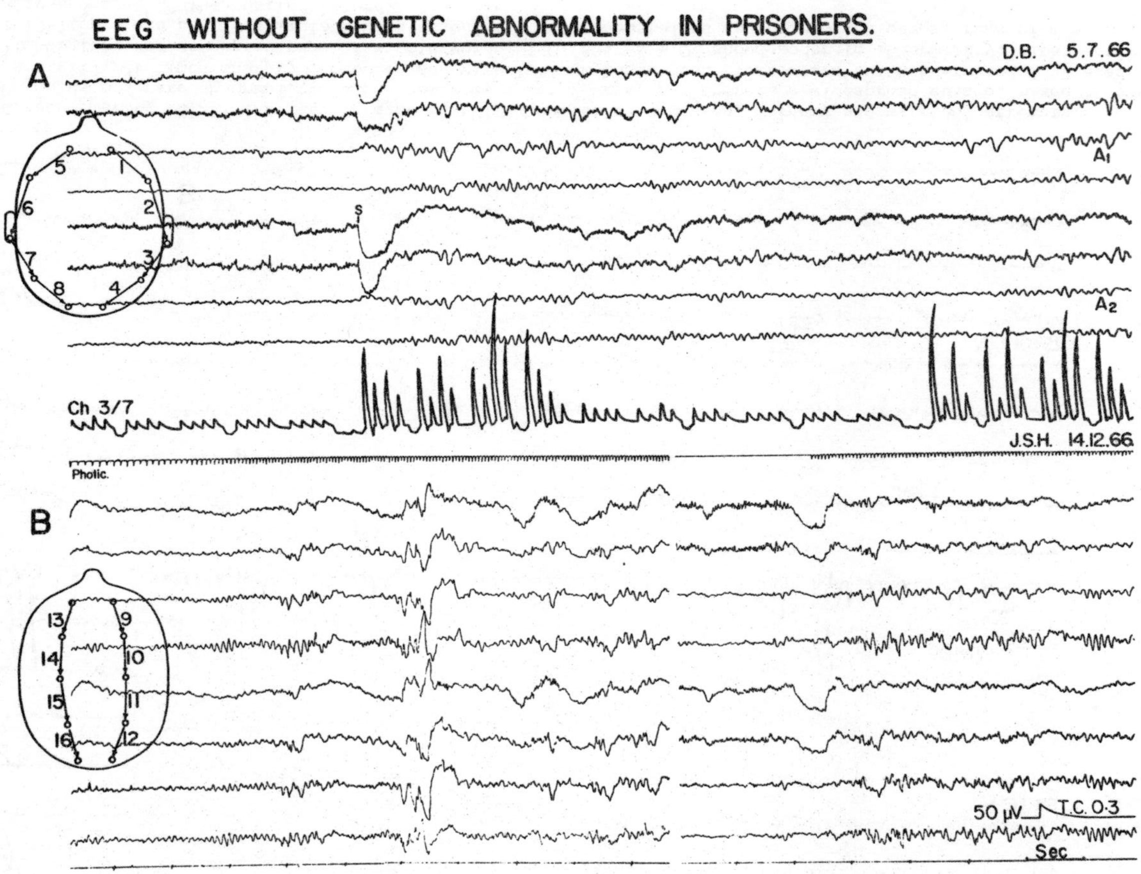

Fig. 3. E.E.G. abnormality in XY inmates. A aged 21; first offence, unprovoked knife attack on a girl; of above average intelligence. E.E.G. shows moderate-severe abnormality; alpha activity is at 6-8 cps and there is a considerable fluctuating excess of slow activity, at times sharply contoured and with right emphasis. (Analyser write-out hand-traced.) B aged 18; larceny and malicious damage; above-average intelligence. E.E.G. shows moderate bilateral slow and sharp wave abnormalities accentuated during photic stimulation, but without paroxysmal symptoms.

MEAN (C.G.) E.E.G. & TREMOR ABUNDANCES: INCIDENCES

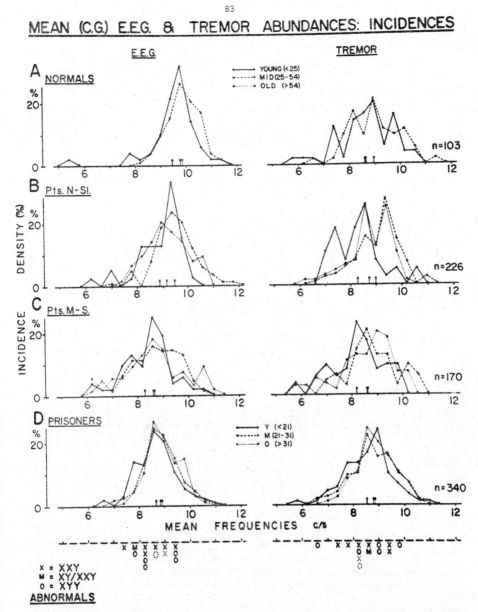

E.E.G.   TREMOR

A NORMALS

— YOUNG (< 25)
•----• MID (25-54)
•·······• OLD (> 54)

n=103

B Pts. N-Sl.

DENSITY (%)

n=226

C Pts. M-S.

INCIDENCE

n=170

D PRISONERS

— Y (< 21)
•----• M (21-31)
•·······• O (> 31)

n=340

MEAN FREQUENCIES c/s

x = XXY
M = XY/XXY
o = XYY
ABNORMALS

Fig. 4. E.E.G. and tremor mean (centre of gravity) frequency values in genetically
abnormal inmates compared with normal and other clinical groups. Normalized
population distributions are shown for (A) normal subjects, (B) general hospital
patients with little E.E.G. abnormality, (C) general patients with moderate or
greater E.E.G. abnormality, (D) Grendon patients. At the bottom are entered the
individual values for the genetically abnormal inmates.* The populations are
shown in 3 age-groups, and mean group values appear on their respective baselines.
Note age ranges are not identical in patient and prisoner groups.

* Two additional cases noted in the addendum have been dotted into this and subsequent
figures.

DOMINANT & MINIMUM E.E.G. ABUNDANCES: INCIDENCES

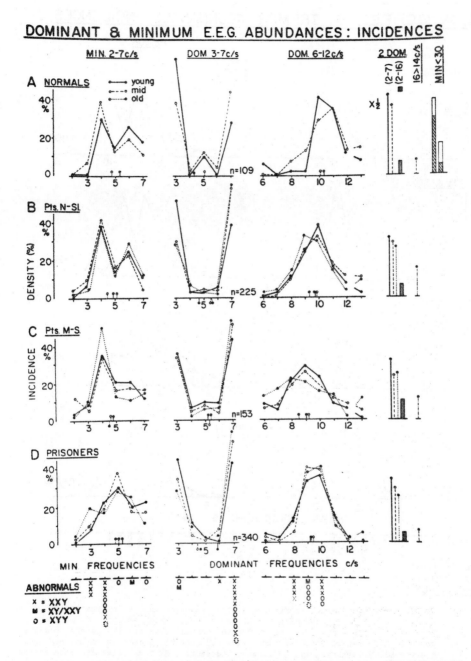

Fig. 5. E.E.G. frequency content in genetically abnormal inmates compared with normal and other clinical groups. Normalized population distributions are shown for the same groups as in Fig. 4, for the three E.E.G. features: minimum in 2-7 cps range, dominant in 3-7 cps range, and dominant in 6-12 cps range. At the bottom are entered the individual genetic case values for the three E.E.G. features.*

* Two additional cases noted in the addendum have been dotted into this and subsequent figures.

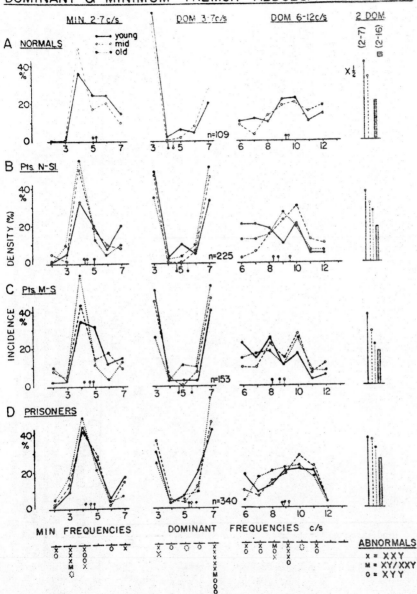

DOMINANT & MINIMUM TREMOR ABDCES.: INCIDENCES

Fig. 6. Tremor frequency content in genetically abnormal patients compared with normal and other clinical groups. Data have been displayed as for Fig. 5.

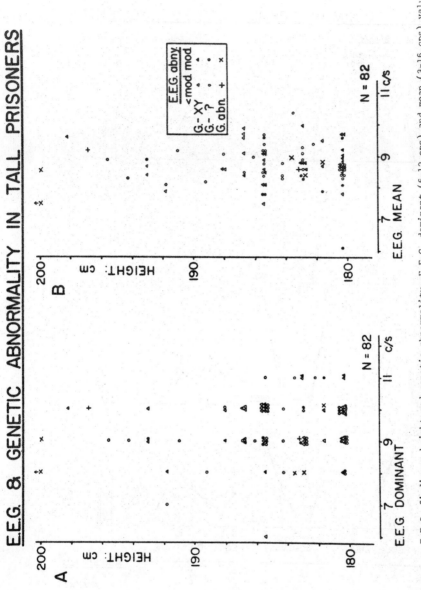

Fig. 7A & B. E.E.G. findings, height and genetic abnormality. E.E.G. dominant (6-12 cps) and mean (3-16 cps) values have each been plotted against height (cms) for the top 25% of inmates (180 cms and over); patients are coded according to E.E.G. abnormality and genetic status. (XY patients with less than moderate abnormality, Δ XY patients with moderate or more abnormality, ▲. Those not genetically checked appear ○ and ● similarly. XYY and XXY patients appear + x.) Two additional cases noted in the addendum have been entered.

FURTHER STUDIES OF 47XYY CONSTITUTION IN PREPUBERTAL CHILD

J. Cowie

The boy (b.21.5.58) was first reported by Cowie and Kahn (1968). Subsequent examinations of his blood showed that he has a chromosome complement of 47,XYY (2 cells having 46 chromosomes with random loss). Chromosome analysis of skin from his left forearm also revealed a chromosome complement of 47,XYY.

He was deemed maladjusted and admitted to a residential school for maladjusted boys after his ninth birthday. The school caters for 50 boys aged 10-16 years. The boys return home at the usual day school holiday times and about every third weekend. Differential behaviour at home and school can be observed. The following is an account of some further investigations and observations since admission to the residential school.

He was his mother's first child and was 11 days postmature. His mother developed toxaemia during the last two months of pregnancy. She was fit and well throughout her second and only other pregnancy. His brother, five years his junior, is developing normally and maintains his growth along the 75th percentile for height according to the criteria of Tanner and Whitehouse. His father is 69 ins. (175 cm.) tall and his mother 64 ins. (163 cm.).

Development

The propositus is growing and developing in accordance with his outsize. His height has increased along the 98th percentile, his sitting height for stature at the 25th percentile and his skinfolds at the 90th percentile.

At the age of 10 years and 9 months there are no signs of pubescence. His genitalia appear relatively small. Both testes are descended and of normal consistency.

General appearance

His face is flushed and at times he sweats profusely. His facies and expression is blank and impassive irrespective of mood. His features are becoming coarser. He has a flattening of his left naso-labial fold, facial asymmetry is becoming more noticeable, and a degree of prognathism is increasing. He has low-set ears and downturned corners of his mouth. He has four café-au-lait patches on his upper limbs. His right hemithorax, arm, leg and foot appear somewhat larger than the left side. His hands are large and equal in size.

Physical examination

Respiratory system is normal.

He has a slow pulse, rarely exceeding 60/min. and well marked sinus arrhythmia. Blood pressure is normal for his years. There is no cardiomegaly and no murmurs on auscaultation. His E.C.G. is within normal limits.

C.N.S. examination reveals no abnormality except a coarse sustained tremor of his outstretched fingers.

His vision (both eyes) is 6/5 and N/5. His fields are full and he has good night vision. Ishihara plates show no colour vision defects. His retinae are so-called "tigroid" in appearance. The macula regions are darker than normal and there is a marked tapetal reflex. There is a slight extension of the medullation of the corneal nerves into the substance of the cornea extending 2 or 3 mm. from the limbus. His parents' and brother's retinae are comparable one to the other and do not show the "tigroid" picture seen in the propositus. Out of the context of the family retinae the XYY retinae might only be considered on the borderline of pigmentary retinopathy at this stage. This would be in line with the finding of McCulloch (1962) applicable to XXY, XXXY, XXX, XO, that no consistent ocular defects were associated with these particular sex chromosome abnormalities and Keith (1968) observes that no ocular abnormalities have been described in XXX and XYY individuals.

X-ray examinations at 10 years

Skull showed no obvious abnormality.

TABLE 1

Ossification centres	Right	Left
Scaphoid	Not appeared; usually present 5-6 years	Just visible
Trapezium	9-10 years	Two tiny centres
Trapezoid	9-10 years	10 years but smaller than right
Fingers	10 years	10 years
Radius	10 years	10 years
Ulna	10 years	10 years
Elbows	10 years	9-10 years. Internal epilondylar O.C. smaller
Hipjoints	The best indication at this age is the epiphysis for the small trochanter, but which is variable in its time of appearance from the 8th to the 14th year. It is not present. The other epiphyseal centres around the hipjoint appear much earlier.	
Knees	10 years	10 years

The X-ray of feet and ankles appear symmetrical and essentially normal except that the epiphyses for the tuberosity of the os calcis was not seen. It is usually well developed by the age of five years.

The bone age according to the carpus varies between $5\frac{1}{2}$ years judging from the scaphoid and 10 years judging from the trapezoid. The bone age as estimated by the radius and ulna epiphyses, fingers and knees is consistent with his chronological age.

Endocrinological investigations

TABLE 2

Age 9 yrs. 5 mths.   Weight 86 lbs. (39 Kg)   Height 58 in. (147 cm)

Blood plasma   Microgrammes/100 ml.

Dehydroepiandrosterone Sulph.	1.27
Dehydroepiandrosterone	138
Testosterone	41
Testosterone Glucuroniside	65
Testosterone Sulphate	5
Androstenedione	Lost during procedure

		T.	A.
Frasier and Horton, Steroids 8,777 (1966):	M Age 4 - 9	42 ± 9	86 ± 12
	F Age 3 - 9	19 ± 8	30 ± 4

TABLE 3

Results microgrammes per 24 hours urinary excretion

	Volume	Testosterone	Epitestosterone
1.	1650 ml	9.0	22.0
2.	1700	7.0	3.5

TABLE 4

	Volume	Oestrone	Oestradiol	Oestriol	17KS	17 OHCS
1.	580	1.4	1.8	14.3	1.8	6.4
2.	520	3.4	3	– (Experiment error)	1.5	6.3

The androgen levels in all samples tested were considered normal in value for a boy of his age. Similarly 17-ketosteroids are about normal. In the two samples in Table 4 the 17 hydroxycorticosteroids are considered to be significantly higher than one would expect. The values for 17 K.S. and 17 OHCS one would expect to be much the same.

Oestrogens

Oestrone and oestradiol are quite low, and in view of this fact not much significance need be attached to the figures. The figure of 14.3 microgrammes per 24 hours for oestriol is a very high one for a boy of his age, and the oestrogen secretion in this sample would not be abnormal for an adult male. The excretion of oestrone and oestriol is usually much the same in amount and considerably higher than that of oestradiol, and therefore the ratio of oestrone: oestradiol: oestriol is somewhat abnormal.

Further analyses showed that the boy's plasma cortisols were perfectly normal with an early morning range of 18 mcg. maximum and 10 mcg. minimum, and a midnight level of 6 mcg. Two separate 24-hour collection for

TABLE 5

Age when assessed	W.I.S.C.			Neale analysis of Reading Ability:			Schonell G.W.S.T.A.	L - R Orientation	Oseretsky Motor Proficiency	Test of Motor Impersistence	Cattell Children's Personality Questionnaire
	Verbal	Perf.	Full Scale	Rate	Accuracy	Compn.					
9y.1m.	75	122	96	7y.4m	7y.0m	7y.3m	5yrs				Deviant on Factor G. Evasive, feels few obligations, weaker superego strength.
10y.0m.	71	120	91	7y.7m	7y.4m	7y.3m	6.1yrs	No evidence of confusion	Average for age	No evidence of impersistence	
10y.8m.	72	113	90	7y.8m	7y.5m	7y.4m	6.3yrs				

urinary steroids showed 17 oxosteroid levels of 3.9 and 5.5 mcg/24 hours
and oxogenic steroids of 10.5 and 10.5. Plasma electrolytes were normal.
His alkaline phosphatase was 20.7 units which is normal for a growing child.
The growth hormone levels were not abnormal.

Intellectual development

Over an eighteen month interval, the W.I.S.C. shows excellent
stability. He was not receiving any medication throughout the assessment
period. The test results and sub-tests are consistent with a diagnosis of
cerebral dysfunctioning affecting language development. His verbal
intelligence is "borderline", whilst his performance estimate is clearly
"superior". The difference of 47 I.Q. points is highly reliable (p<.001)
and abnormal, 0.1% of the population of boys of this age obtaining such a
difference.

Educationally, minimal progress is being made. In class he is
amenable to discipline and shows good concentration when working in the
handicraft class. This reflects his high performance skills. Relative to
age, however, he is severely retarded at least in basic school attainments,
which is probably not inconsistent with his level of verbal intelligence.
His spelling is very weak and he has difficulty in associating the sound
with the written word.

In school his behaviour is unexceptional. He will evade rules given
the opportunity; he feels few obligations and conforms because it is
expedient to do so.

At home during the holidays he quickly reverts to former patterns of
absconding, stealing and defying parental authority. Outbursts of
aggression are no longer apparent. His parents appear to expect him to
repeat earlier patterns and the boy obliges them.

Observations and investigations of cerebral functioning

It has been observed that he has episodes of unexplained hyperpyrexia
when his temperature fluctuates between 97% and 99%. When he has a mild
infection, his temperature rises to above 100°F and during a severe
infection, a recording of 104.5^{o}F was reached before his fever responded to
treatment. In view of this an investigation of his thermoregulatory
functions was made. No definite abnormality was demonstrated in either
thermoregulatory or subjective responses to heat or to cold. It was
considered, however, that these normal findings do not rule out an epileptic
kind of disturbance involving the thermoregulatory centres as a cause of
his short-lived elevations of body temperature. When his fever is high he
becomes derealized and persons appear to be bigger. He has illusions of
people entering his room through the walls instead of the doors.

At times his coarse hand tremor becomes more noticeable and momentary
shivers ripple down his body.

More dramatic attacks have been observed in which he has an aura of
dizziness and of the floor appearing to sway and then spin. He describes
that he feels that there is "nasty irritating stuff" in his nose. During
an attack he has been observed blowing his nose vigorously for a few
seconds then staggering about, his body sagging and knees giving way. He
falls if not supported, and he does not respond to or understand commands.
He looks flushed and hot, and his temperature is raised to above 99°F. He
recovers in about 10 minutes and his temperature returns to normal within
half an hour following such an attack.

He is a restless sleeper and occasionally wets his bed.

E.E.G. studies

Family E.E.G. studies show that the father, aged 38, the mother, aged 34, and brother, aged 8 years, all have stable records.

The propositus had serial E.E.Gs. done when alert, when fasting, after food, during natural sleep and during barbiturate-induced sleep.

When alert, a high voltage somewhat irregular 9 C/S alpha was observed over the posterior head region on both sides spreading further forward. Mixed with it were some theta elements and more strikingly some sharply contoured delta waves, particularly over the temporal regions. These were somewhat more obvious on the right than on the left. Also on the right were some brief high voltage rhythmic runs of delta. With the eyes open the background rhythms described were attenuated. Over the anterior parts of the head, apart from spreading alpha, there were episodes of rhythmic theta and rhythmic delta.

Overbreathing caused a slight increase in the amount of slow activity; it certainly did not accentuate the repetitive spike discharges.

As he became drowsy, background rhythms became attenuated and high-voltage left-temporal spikes appeared repetitively. Sleep phenomena such as V waves and spindles occurred episodically, as did the sudden appearance of alpha rhythms with external stimuli. On a few occasions there were bursts of notched generalised high-voltage delta activity. As the recording proceeded, the spikes became more frequent and more widespread and a check was made to show that they were not cardiographic artefact. They appeared to take origin in the middle and posterior temporal region on the left side and were never seen on the right.

Barbiturate-induced sleep. Twenty minutes after 100 mgms. quinal barbitone (seconal), the E.E.G. showed pick-up of barbiturate fast waves equally in the right and left fronto-temporal areas. There was complete suppression of sharp waves in the left fronto-temporal area during seconal-induced sleep.

This suggests that the sharp waves can be suppressed by barbiturate at the equivalent stage of sleep where the sharp waves were discharging during the natural sleep.

The normal pick-up of barbiturate fast activity in the left fronto-temporal area suggests absence of gross atrophic anatomical damage.

After 4 weeks on phenobarbitone 100 mgm. at 21.00 hours. E.E.G. at mid-day: no sharp waves seen in alert E.E.G. record, and no sharp waves occurred during either lighter or deeper natural sleep.

Dermatoglyphics

Reports on the dermatoglyphics of the XYY are very few and limited to isolated cases. As yet there are no specific dermatoglyphic peculiarities attributed to the chromosomal anomaly. Dermatoglyphic standards are arrived at statistically for populations and not for individuals. Because of the paucity of available data it was considered worthwhile to place on record the dermatoglyphics of this boy and his family.

Table 6. FAMILY DERMATOGLYPHICS

NAME		LEFT V	LEFT IV	LEFT III	LEFT II	LEFT I	RIGHT I	RIGHT II	RIGHT III	RIGHT IV	RIGHT V	TOTAL RIDGE COUNT LEFT	TOTAL RIDGE COUNT RIGHT
PROPOSITUS		U^{16}	W^I	TL^{UI}	RI / T	TL^{UI}	TL^{UI}	LP^I / R^{13}	W^I	W^M	U^{15}	–	–
		16–0	12/22	11/14	1–0	14/18	17/15	3/13	11/20	20/15	15–0	54/54	66/63
FATHER		U^{22}	W^I	W^M	TL^{RO}	scar W	W^I	TL^{RI}	W^M	W^M	TL^{UO}	–	–
		22–0	17/19	17/19	19/7	20/26	18/23	over 8/30	15/16	17/16	20/11	95/71	78/96
MOTHER		abt U^{16}	U^{21}	U^{17}	W^O	TL^{UI}	U^{19}	W^I	U^{17}	W^O	U^{15}	–	–
		16–0	21–0	14–19	11–15	19–0	19–0	12–16	17–0	over 23–12	15–0	81/34	86/28
BROTHER		U^{21}	over W^I	U^{17}	W^O	TL^{UI}	$TL\,R^{I/M}$ $TL\,R^I$	scar $TL\,RI$ / W	U^{17}	TL^{RI}	U^{24}	–	–
		21–0	16–27	17–0	22–19	16–21	22–25	abt abt 16–26	17–0	23–22	24–0	92/67	102/73

CODE:– T–Tented Arch. U–Ulnar Loop. R–Radial Loop. W–Whorl. TL–Twinned Loop.
LP–Lateral Pocket Loop. I–Inner Tracing. M–Meeting Tracing. O–Outer Tracing.

FATHER

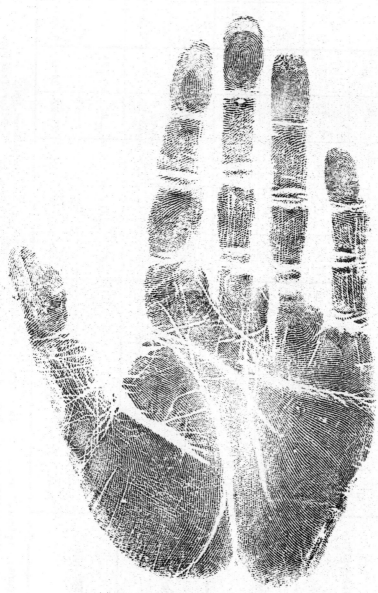

FATHER

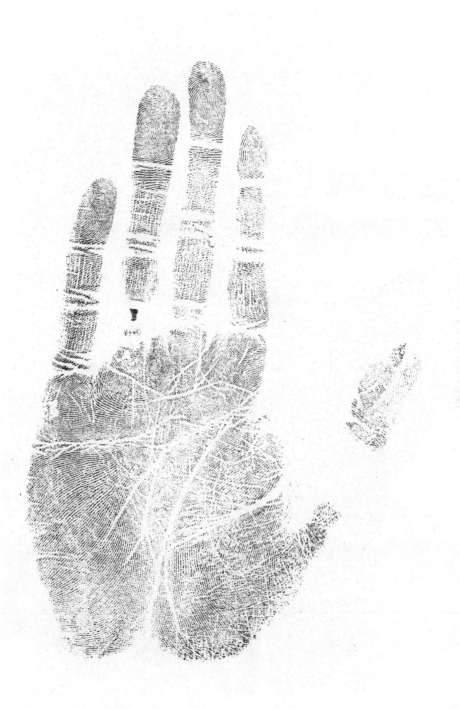

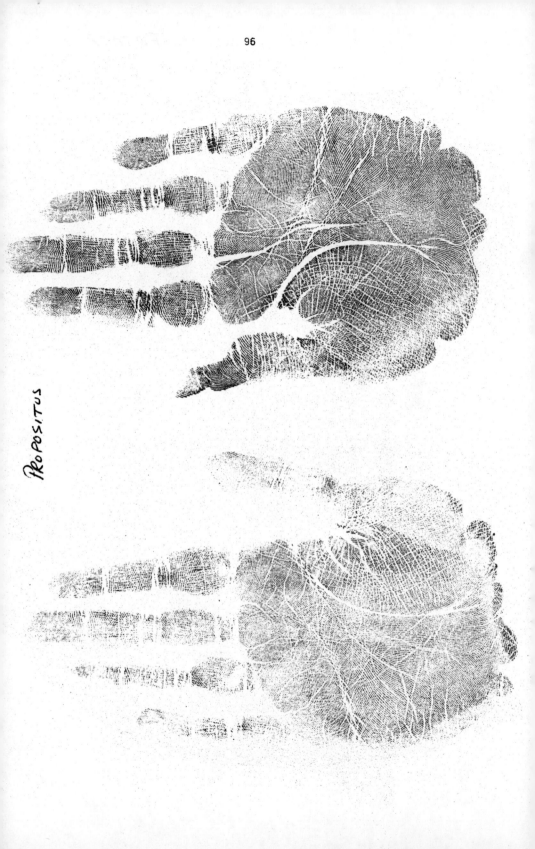

PROPOSITUS

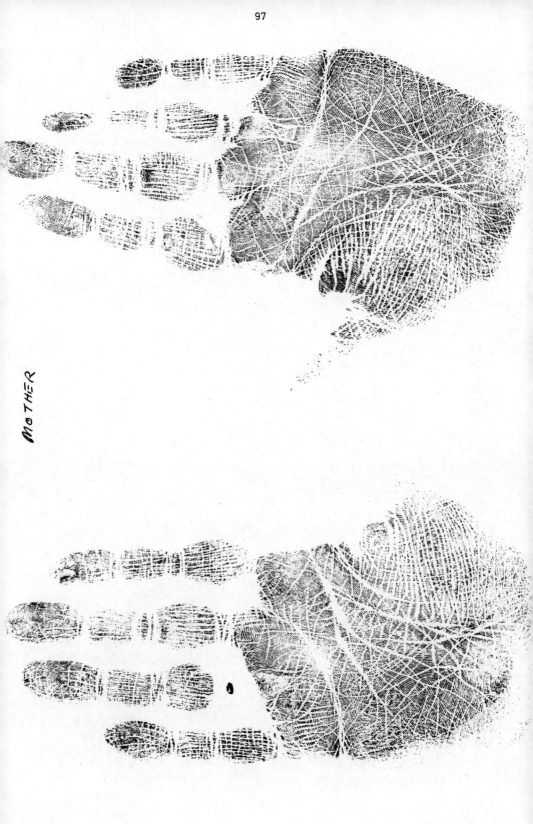

MOTHER

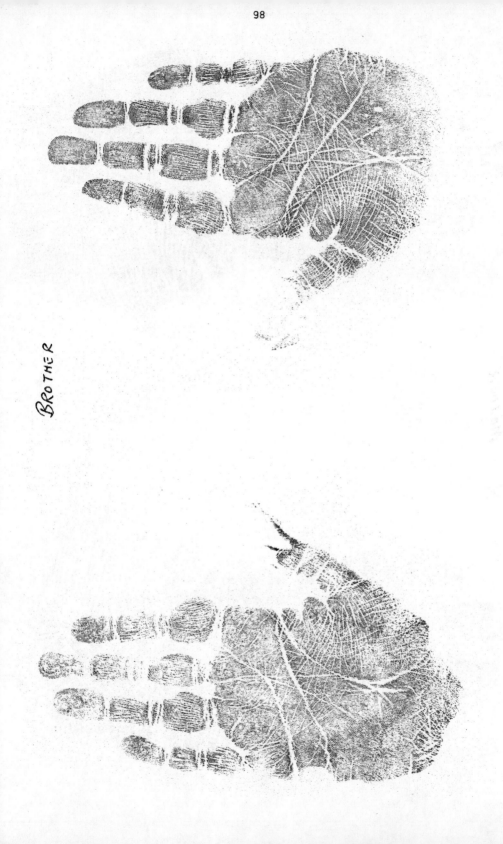

BROTHER

The propositus has by far much lower finger ridge count than either his parents or his sibling. He does not have as many patterns in his palms as the rest of his family. The ridges of the palms fall into the usual patterns with the exception of those in the area between the left thenar and base of left forefinger where a distinct and unusual pattern has been formed.

Summary

Further studies of a prepubertal boy with an XYY constitution are described. No evidence of mosaicism is revealed on chromosomal analysis of blood and skin from one forearm.

Serial E.E.G. studies show left-sided temporal spike discharging foci becoming evident during natural sleep. The spikes are not seen during barbiturate-induced sleep.

His height growth is maintained along the 98th percentile. Radiography reveals retardation, acceleration and asymmetry of bone maturation.

Biochemical analysis shows normal androgen levels in urine and plasma. The oestrogen secretions in samples of urine taken at the age of 9 years would be considered normal for an adult male and the ratio of oestrone : oestradiol : oestriol is somewhat abnormal.

There is a wide discrepancy between verbal and performance abilities, and some of his intellectual and personality difficulties could possibly be explained by his cerebral dysfunctioning.

An analysis of family dermatoglyphics is reported.

Acknowledgements

I acknowledge with gratitude assistance from many sources.

I am particularly indebted to Mr. Eric Thomas, headmaster of Starhurst Residential School, to his staff, Dr. W.A. Young and to Mr. G.R. Crowther, Educational Psychologist.

My special thanks are due to Dr. A. Stuart Mason for endocrinological and other in-patient investigations, including thermoregulatory functioning assessments by Dr. W.R. Keatinge and electroencephalography by Dr. D.R. Scott. Serial E.E.G. studies were carried out by Dr. E.D. West, endocrinological studies by Dr. Margaret Stern and Dr. B.W.L. Brooksbank; chromosomal analysis by Professor P.E. Polani, eye studies by Mr. Ian Duguid; radiography by Drs. A.S. Craner, E.B. Davies and S. Murray.

I am grateful for the willing co-operation of Chief Inspector Bentley of the Finger Print Department of New Scotland Yard for recording and analysing the family dermatoglyphics.

CHROMOSOME ABNORMALITY AND LEGAL ACCOUNTABILITY

J.E. Hall Williams

Chromosome abnormality

A review of the scientific literature concerning chromosome abnormalities suggests that while certain difficulties exist concerning the nature of the scientific evidence, wide claims are being made about its relevance to legal responsibility, and in particular to criminal responsibility, which it is the purpose of this paper to examine.

The difficulties referred to involve uncertainties and contradictions in the scientific results which may or may not be capable of resolution. These appear to be as follows:-

1. **The incidence of abnormal chromosome counts in the normal population is not yet established.** It is said to be as follows (Telfer *et al.*, 1968, p.1250):

    1 in 2,000 of extra Y chromosomes in adult males;
    1 in 500 of extra X chromosomes in adult males;
    1 in 80 of tall American males.

    Among male live births, it seems that the frequency of chromatin-positive males, or males with an abnormal nuclear sex, is about 1.7 per 1,000. As the identification has been by nuclear sexing, these abnormal males are those with more than one X chromosome (Court Brown *et al.*,1968a, p.181). It is further suggested that the XXY condition is found in about 1.3 per 1,000 live births. All other abnormalities are very rare at birth.

2. **The relation with subnormality is not clear.**

    Abnormal chromosomes are found in 9.4 per 1,000 males in hospitals for the mentally subnormal, or between five and six times as frequently as in liveborn male babies (Court Brown *et al.*, 1968a, p.183). But there is evidence that among the most retarded cases, 'the frequency of abnormal males is not materially different from that among the liveborn male population, while there is about a ninefold increase among the high-grade mentally subnormal, of whom, on average, about one male in sixty-five has an abnormal nuclear sex' (Court Brown *et al.*, 1968a, pp.183-4).

3. **Some confusion is caused by the failure to maintain a clear distinction between evidence concerning extra X chromosome cases and evidence concerning extra Y chromosome cases.**

    Yet it seems there are important differences between the extra X and the extra Y cases. Some of the research concerns one type rather than the other. Some of the research involves both types. Further confusion is caused by the tendency to limit discussion of chromosome abnormalities to a consideration of these two types, to the exclusion of other chromosome abnormalities.

    Dr. Casey's study suggests that, among patients in state hospitals at Rampton and Moss Side, an unusually large proportion of men had an extra X chromosome. They tended to have abnormal physical features (Casey *et al.*, 1966b).

    The Telfer study of inmates of four institutions revealed seven out of 129 subjects with the extra X component, and five with the extra Y (Telfer *et al.*, 1968).

Patricia Jacobs and co-workers found at Carstairs state hospital about three per cent of men with an extra Y component. The XYY males are normally developed physically (Court Brown *et al.*, 1968a, p.189-190).

4. The differences observed include differences in the direction of the anti-social or criminal behaviour.

Extra Y males are not so likely to commit aggressive sexual crimes as the extra X males, the tendency being for them to commit crimes against property rather than offences against the person (Court Brown *et al.*, 1968a, p.191).

The average age of commencement of a criminal career is said to be earlier in the case of extra Y patients (Price and Whatmore, 1967a). Nervous disabilities (Richard Daly, 1969b) and severe personality disorders (Price and Whatmore, 1967a) are reported among these patients. The controls used by Price and Whatmore exhibited more open aggression and were more often hostile and violent.

The legal cases, where extra Y chromosome complement has been raised, all involved homicide or acts of aggression. (These cases are discussed below.)

5. It cannot be claimed that general surveys of delinquent populations reveal a high.proportion of chromosome abnormality.

The evidence for this is slight. Only three out of 607 males sentenced to borstal training in Scotland in a twelve-month period in 1966 and 1967 were found to be chromatin-positive. (Jacobs *et al.* quoted in Court Brown *et al.*, 1968a, p.187). Four studies taken together reveal no significant proportion of abnormal males in the delinquent populations studied (Court Brown *et al.*, 1968a, p.188).

But Telfer gives figures indicating a high proportion of abnormality among tall American males in correctional facilities. This may be explained by the concentration on tallness (Telfer *et al.*, 1968).

Legal accountability

Putting the claims at their highest, it is said that:

i. There is no doubt about the correlation between the double Y chromosome, criminality and anti-social behaviour, increasing in frequency with decreasing intelligence (Nielsen, 1968a).

ii. It is possible that the patients' personality deviation and criminality were due to the sex chromosome constitution of XYY (Nielsen, 1968a).

iii. The patients being genetically disposed to criminality are unlikely to respond to punishment (Nielsen, 1968a).

iv. The extra Y chromosome has resulted in a severely disordered personality, and this disorder has led these men into conflict with the law (Price and Whatmore, 1967a).

v. There is no reason to believe that these men would have indulged in crime had it not been for their abnormal personalities (Price and Whatmore, 1967a).

vi. Males with an extra Y chromosome studied in the special hospitals 'suffered a severe disorder of personality, in most instances associated with some degree of intellectual impairment'. It seems that 'their intellectual function may have been insufficient to suppress the disordered drives leading to criminal behaviour' (Anthony

Allison, 1969). 'The inheritance of an extra Y chromosome has resulted in a severely disordered personality, which has led these men into conflict with the law' (Anthony Allison, 1969).

We shall now examine the application of the criminal law to the subject, in the light of the above claims made about its significance.

The application of the criminal law

Evidence of abnormal chromosome complements may be relevant to the application of the criminal law at any one of five stages:

1. unfitness to be the subject of proceedings;
2. fitness to plead;
3. the insanity defence;
4. diminished responsibility;
5. disposal under the Mental Health Act 1959 after conviction.

1 and 2. Fitness for trial

The relevance of evidence of an extra X or extra Y chromosome in the case of either unfitness to be the subject of criminal proceedings or, if the subject is committed to trial, on the issue of fitness to plead, must be slight. The tests applied here are the suitability of the subject to stand up to the normal criminal procedures, and the ability to comprehend the trial, instruct his legal representatives and the like. It is suggested that few cases of chromosome abnormalities would appear to be coupled with such serious personality disorder as to make it impossible to try the person, or to make the question of fitness to plead a real issue. It would be interesting to know how many of the cases observed in the state hospitals had been sent there as being unfit to plead or to be tried. There is evidence that in Scotland this device is used more frequently than in England and Wales. At least the Royal Commission on Capital Punishment reported to that effect in 1953 (*Report*, Cmd. 8932, p.89).

3. The insanity defence

It is conceived that few of the extra chromosome cases could establish that because of this characteristic they satisfied the requirements of the M'Naghten Rules relating to the defence of insanity. These are either one of the following two conditions, stemming from a disease of the mind:

i. he did not know what he was doing;
ii. he did not know that it was wrong, i.e. against the law.

The more retarded subjects might be able to satisfy the second limb of the Rules in extreme cases, and occasionally the first limb would be satisfied. But evidence of an extra chromosome would not of itself lead to such a conclusion. It should be used as part of the evidence leading a medical witness to conclude that there was a disorder which satisfied the Rules.

The use of the M'Naghten Rules has declined dramatically since the introduction of diminished responsibility into English law in 1957. It now seems that many cases which might previously have squeezed by under the M'Naghten Rules are dealt with by the alternative method, which we must now examine.

4. Diminished responsibility

The cases decided under section 2 of the Homicide Act 1957 show that a pretty wide range of behaviour may be recognised as coming within the purview of diminished responsibility. No doubt some courts would be

prepared to listen to evidence of an extra chromosome complement as part of
the medical history of a case. The touchstone of the defence is substantial
impairment of mental responsibility, which must be arising from a condition
of arrested or retarded development of mind or from some inherent cause, or
be induced by disease or injury. This is intended to rule out crimes of
passion, or indulgence in violence which is not pathologically induced.
To use Lord Devlin's phrase, when as a trial judge he dealt with *Kemp*,
[1956] 3 W.L.R. 724, it is not intended to apply to 'brutish stupidity
without rational power', where there is not mental illness or subnormality
to explain it. Evidence of subnormality coupled with evidence of the
extra chromosome complement could lead a medical witness to conclude that
there was substantial impairment of responsibility within the meaning of
section 2, Homicide Act 1957. But once again we must stress that the extra
chromosome complement by itself does not establish this. It is also to be
noted that few of the extra Y chromosome types commit acts of violence or
aggression. The direction of their crimes lies more often in the property
field. It should be remembered that the defence of diminished responsibility
is so far limited to cases of homicide.

5. Sentence stage

At the sentence stage, after a finding of guilt or responsibility,
extra chromosome evidence may be relevant in two ways:

a) In mitigation of penalty. Here it is conceived that any evidence
of this nature could be used to show that the crime may be regarded as no
more than an expression of the distorted personality, and a more or less
inevitable consequence of it. However, it should be realised that no one
has yet clearly demonstrated that the extra chromosome inevitably leads to
crime. Comparison between the incidence in the normal population and the
incidence in special hospitals, and penal institutions, does no more than
demonstrate a higher probability of finding persons with extra chromosomes
in an abnormal hospital or delinquent population. Such findings hardly
warrant the more extreme statements noted above.

b) The second way in which the extra chromosome may be relevant on
sentence is by way of persuading the court to exercise its powers under
the Mental Health Act 1959. These powers allow the court to make a
hospital order or guardianship order under section 60, with or without a
restriction order under section 65. The evidence required is of a mental
disorder within the meaning of the Act, that is to say, mental illness,
psychopathic disorder, subnormality or severe subnormality; and this must
be of a nature or degree which warrants the detention of the patient in a
hospital for medical treatment, or his reception into guardianship under
the Act. The court must then, before making an order, form the opinion
that this is the most suitable method of disposing of the case, having
regard to all the circumstances, including the nature of the offence, and
the character and antecedents of the offender, and to the other available
methods of dealing with him. In addition the court must be satisfied
that arrangements have been made for the admission of an offender to a
hospital, if that is what is proposed, within a period of twenty-eight
days, or, where guardianship is proposed, that the authority or person
designated to act as guardian is willing to receive the offender into
guardianship.

No doubt hospital orders will frequently be made in the case of
subnormal offenders, where the evidence shows an extra chromosome. The
medical witnesses may properly take evidence concerning this factor into
account in making their recommendations. The question which may be asked
is whether this information will be available at this stage. Unless the
person has been remanded for a medical report, the prison authorities may
not have had time to carry out the necessary tests. Another question is

whether they have the facilities. It is suggested that defence lawyers should be alerted to the desirability of obtaining evidence about the chromosome complement of any client who is unusually tall, and of subnormal intelligence. This is especially desirable where there is a history of failure to respond to normal sanctions. For the scientific literature suggests that persons with an extra chromosome are slow to respond to punishment. Nielsen (1968a) says (p.201): 'It seems unlikely that punishment of any kind would change the risk of new crimes in patients who are genetically disposed to criminality, as, for instance, patients with the sex chromosome constitution XYY or patients with Klinefelter's syndrome and the sex chromosome constitution XXY'. A hospital or guardianship order might be more suitable than prison for such cases.

The reform of the legal tests

Nielsen suggests that special provision should be made for the sentencing of persons who are genetically disposed to criminality with no, or at least very little, possibility of cure or correction (1968a, p.201). The legal tests of accountability have long been regarded as unsatisfactory in relation to abnormal mental conditions. With the abolition of capital punishment, the pressure to reform the M'Naghten Rules, or to use them, has declined; and since 1957 diminished responsibility has provided a flexible and attractive alternative for homicide cases. But will the Law Commission, which is now drawing up a code of general principles of criminal law, be content to leave the matter thus? There is considerable force in the argument that the whole question of insanity should be postponed to be dealt with at the sentence stage, after the finding of guilt (see, for example, Goldstein and Katz, 1963). This solution, which might be coupled with the assimilation of the disposal provisions with the Mental Health Act provisions, leaving it optional for the judge to make a hospital order or to order a special hospital committal, has at first sight many attractions. But it fails to deal with two vital points:

i. The relevance of mental disorder to intent (or *mens rea*, to use the lawyers' phrase). If the person is so deranged that he could not form the intention to commit the crime (a somewhat rare case, admittedly) - in the sense that he did not act deliberately and did not know what he was doing - would the reformers be content if he were acquitted?

ii. Does not the present law involve the jury's participating in an important and vital decision, namely, who is to be found responsible and who is to be excused on the grounds of mental disorder, whereas the other solution removes from the jury's purview the whole question of mental responsibility?

Professor A.S. Goldstein (1967) has suggested that there is a superficial plausibility about the proposal to abolish the insanity defence, but that there are 'a great many objections' to doing so (p.222). He says that one of these is that the proposal 'tends to sweep past the jury and toward the sentencing stage large numbers of offenders who would now go free', and has the effect of tucking away in an administrative process 'the vitally important distinction between illness and evil'. He argues that the insanity defence plays an important part in reinforcing the notion of criminal responsibility in our society. To undermine or eliminate it at the present time would involve certain risks and might be harmful to society's interests.

A reform which might be easier to accept, though it might have little practical effect, would be to extend the diminished responsibility defence to cover other crimes apart from homicide. The objection to this is that at present, in these other crimes, evidence of diminished responsibility can always be used in mitigation of punishment or to procure a hospital order. The only purpose of introducing the defence would be to alter the category of the crime committed, which is what now happens when murder is reduced to manslaughter. Is there a case for allowing the category of the crime committed to be reduced on the ground of diminished responsibility? Some argue that in crimes such as aggravated assaults the proof of diminished responsibility could be used to reduce the offence to ordinary assault. This would be a rather limited reform of little significance. The better view may well be that we should reform the insanity defence by replacing it with diminished responsibility, as a general defence to all crime, and see how this works out in practice. There might be something to be said for this solution, not only on the technical ground that the M'Naghten Rules are outmoded and inappropriate, but also to get away from the mandatory consequences of a special verdict viz. indefinite detention at the discretion of the Secretary of State. In other words, we should let the court use its Mental Health Act powers not only where a person is convicted but also where he is found to be suffering from diminished responsibility by verdict of the jury, and on that ground is acquitted or convicted of a lesser crime. At present the powers of the courts are only exercisable following the conviction of an offender (or, exceptionally, by magistrates' courts when they are satisfied that an offence has been committed but without proceeding to a conviction). What is here proposed is a new power similar to that which has been conferred upon the Court of Appeal when allowing an appeal against an insanity verdict, viz. when substituting a verdict of acquittal, to couple with it an order for the admission of the appellant to a mental hospital for observation, where the court thinks that this is desirable in the interests of the appellant's own health or safety or with a view to the protection of other persons. It may be quite unrealistic to suggest that a power which is acceptable when dealing with an appellant who succeeds with his appeal can be extended to cover all cases of acquittal, where the court might have reason to believe that the public interest or the accused person's own interest required a period of observation in a mental hospital.

This discussion has not dealt with the question whether a special section should be provided in the law dealing with persons who are genetically disposed to criminality. It is submitted that questions concerning the mental disposition or predisposition to criminality must find their place, if they can, within the confines of a restatement of the general rules about legal accountability in cases of mental abnormality. This is why we have examined those rules and the possible directions of any reforms. There is no room in the law for a special section dealing exclusively with the extra chromosome situation.

The case law concerning abnormal chromosomes

There are a few unreported cases where the defence in a criminal trial has apparently raised the question of abnormal chromosomes. The cases may be classified according to the way in which the matter was resolved.

a) As part of the evidence proving the insanity defence

The Australian case of *Lawrence Hannell*, a 21 year-old packer who murdered his 77 year-old landlady, was a case where the psychiatrists gave evidence of their conclusion that Hannell was insane within the legal test. Part of their evidence was the fact that Hannell had an extra Y chromosome. It is not clear from the transcript that the chromosome aberration had any bearing on the finding of insanity. Clearly there was other evidence to that effect. Hannell was found to be insane and was ordered to be detained at the Governor's pleasure (Sergovich, 1969, p.304).

In New York, in the trial of *Sean Farley*, aged 26, for the murder of a 49-year-old woman, a geneticist testified that the accused had an extra Y chromosome. He said the presence of extra Y's in the defendant's pattern had been found to be associated with extreme tallness and aggressiveness, but he did not agree with the defence lawyer's suggestion that the extra Y was necessarily related to antisocial or criminal behaviour. 'It can contribute', he is reported as saying, 'but by itself it would not be a factor'. Farley was found guilty of first degree murder. (25 April 1969, newspaper report.)

In Bielefeld, Western Germany, in November 1968, one *Ernst-Dieter Beck*, a 20-year-old farm worker, was sentenced to life imprisonment for the murder of three women. Scientific evidence was given that Beck had an extra Y chromosome and that this made him unable to control his impulses to commit crimes, including the present murders. The prosecution's view was that Beck was fully aware that he was committing murder even though he might not have been able to control his impulse to kill, and that he should therefore be held responsible. This appears to have been the view of the court, for Beck was found guilty and sentenced to life imprisonment (Fox, unpublished lecture).

b) In mitigation of punishment

The French case of the stablehand, *Daniel Heugon*, who was accused of the murder of a prostitute in a Paris hotel, is an example of a case where the abnormal chromosome complement was used in mitigation of punishment. After a suicide attempt in his cell he was chromosome-tested and found to have an extra Y chromosome. Evidence was offered at the trial that this might be a mitigating factor, and the accused received a reduced sentence of seven years imprisonment (*Observer*, 24 March 1968; Sergovich, 1969, 303-4).

c) On appeal

In the case of *Richard Speck*, the American who was convicted of murdering eight Chicago nurses, it was reported that the defence attorneys intended to plead on appeal that he had an extra Y chromosome. (*Observer*, 24 March 1968; Sergovich, 1969, p.304). The Illinois Supreme Court in November 1968 upheld Speck's conviction for murder as well as the death sentence imposed upon him. Fox says that the fact of his chromosome abnormality was not part of the defence case at the trial nor was it raised at subsequent appeals (Fox, unpublished lecture).

In Los Angeles it was reported in March 1968 that a United States superior court judge had denied a motion on behalf of one *Raymond S. Tanner*, aged 33, who wished to appeal against his conviction for assault with intent to murder, arising out of his having raped a woman in 1967 and beaten her. Tanner's counsel argued that the extra chromosome 'predestined' Tanner to aggressive behaviour and uncontrollable impulses, and that he was entitled to an insanity verdict. The judge ruled that there was insufficient evidence to prove any relationship between the 'XYY syndrome' and human behaviour.*

d) As ground for the excercise of the prerogative of mercy

In 1961 in Australia, *Robert Peter Tait* murdered an elderly woman who caught him in the act of housebreaking; he was at the time on parole for assaulting a 70-year-old woman. He was caught and tried. At the trial for murder, his plea of insanity failed and he was sentenced to death. After considerable delay, during which public pressure for his reprieve mounted, the sentence of death was commuted. Tait, who had exhibited

* Information supplied to the author by Dr. John Cowie, based on a newspaper report, March 7, 1968.

considerable signs of sexual deviance both at the time of the murder and previously, was subsequently found to have an abnormal XYY complement. This came to light in a chromosome survey conducted at Melbourne's Pentridge Prison. It is suggested by Fox that had this fact been known at the time of the trial and the subsequent public controversy surrounding the case, while it would have made no difference to the rejection of the plea of insanity, it might have led to a speedier commutation of the death penalty (Fox, unpublished lecture).

Conclusion

It is submitted that these cases support the arguments advanced above about the way in which evidence of abnormal chromosome complement may be used in criminal trials.

BIBLIOGRAPHY

1 Akesson, H.O., Forssman, H. & Wallin, L. (1968) Chromosomes of tall men in mental hospitals. *Lancet*, 2, 1040

2 Akesson, H.O., Forssman, H. & Wallin, L. (1969). Gross chromosomal errors in tall men admitted to mental hospitals. *Acta psychiat. scand.*, 45, 37

3 Allison, A. (1969). Genes and population. In Paterson, D. (ed.) *Genetic engineering* (B.B.C. Public.), 54.

4 Anderson, I.F., Goeller, M.A. & Wallace, C. (1964). Sex chromosome abnormalities in a population of 1,662 mental defectives. *S. Afr. med. jo.*, 38, 346

5 Baikie, A.G., Garson, O.M., Weste, S.M. & Ferguson, J. (1966). Numerical abnormalities of the X chromosome. *Lancet*, 1, 398

6 Balodimos, M., Lisco, H., Irwin, I., Merrill, W. & Dingman, J.F. (1966). XYY karyotype in a case of familial hypogonadism. *Jo. clin. endocrin.*, 26, 443

7 Barr, M.L. & Carr, D.H. (1962). Correlations between sex chromatin and sex chromosomes. *Acta cytol.* [Philad.], 6, 34

8 Barr, M.L., Shaver, E.L., Carr, D.H. & Plunkett, E.R. (1959). An unusual sex chromatin pattern in three mentally deficient subjects. *Jo. ment. defic. res.*, 3, 78

9 Barr, M.L., Shaver, E.L., Carr, D.H. & Plunkett, E.R. (1960). The chromatin-positive Klinefelter's syndrome among patients in mental deficiency hospitals. *Jo. ment. defic. res.*, 4, 89

10 Bartholomew, A.A. (1968). The extra Y chromosome and criminal behaviour. *Aust. N.Z. jo. psychiatry*, 2, 6

11 Bartholomew, A.A. (1969). A defence of insanity and the extra Y chromosome *Aust. N.Z. jo. psychiatry*, 2, (1), 29

12 Bartlett, D.J., Hurley, W.P., Brand, C.R. and Poole, E.W. (1968). Chromosomes of male patients in a security prison. *Nature* [Lond.], 219, 351

13 Berg, J.M., Faunch, J.A., Pendrey, M.J., Penrose, L.S., Ridler, M.A.C. & Shapiro, A. (1969). A homozygous chromosomal variant. *Lancet*, 1, 531

14 Bergman, S., Bjersing, L. & Reitalu, J. (1963). A mentally defective male with Klinefelter's syndrome and probable XXYY/XXY mosaicism. *Cytogenetics*, 2, 280

15 Bergman, S., Reitalu, J., Nowakowski, H. & Lanz, W. (1960). The chromosomes in two patients with Klinefelter syndrome. *Ann. hum. genet.* 24, 81

16 Bertrand, C.M., de Grouchy, J., Blondet, P. & Royer, P. (1964). Syndrome de Turner avec 47 chromosomes dont XY est un chromosome surnuméraire. *Ann. endocrin.* [Paris], 25, 441

17 Biesele, J.J., Schmid, W. & Lawlis, M.G. (1962). Mentally retarded schizoid twin girls with 47 chromosomes. *Lancet*, 1, 403

18 Borgaonkar, D.S., Murdoch, J.L., McKusick, V.A., Borkowf, B.P. & Money, J.W. (1968). The YY syndrome. *Lancet*, 2, 461

19 Breg, W.R., Castilla, E.E., Miller, O.J. & Cornwell, J.G. (1963). Sex chromatin and chromosome studies in 1,562 institutionalized mental defectives. *Jo. pediat.*, 63, 738

20 British Medical Journal. (1967). Criminal behaviour and the Y chromosome. *Brit. med. jo.*, 1, 64

21 British Medical Journal [Legal correspondent] (1968) Abnormal chromosome. *Brit. med. jo.*, 4, 398

22 British Medical Journal (1969). An English XYY murder trial (leading article). *Brit. med. jo.*, 1, 201

23 Carakushansky, G., Neu, R.L. & Gardner, L.I. (1968). XYY with abnormal genitalia. *Lancet*, 2, 1144

24 Casey, M.D., Blank, C.E., Street, D.R.K., Segall, L.J., McDougall, J.H., McGrath, P.J. & Skinner, J.L. (1966a). YY chromosomes and antisocial behaviour. *Lancet*, 2, 859

25 Casey, M.D., Segall, L.J., Street, D.R.K. & Blank, C.E., (1966b). Sex chromosome abnormalities in two state hospitals for patients requiring special security. *Nature* [Lond.], 209, 641

26 Casey, M.D., Street, D.R.K., Segall, L.J. & Blank, C.E. (1968). Patients with sex chromatin abnormality in two state hospitals. *Ann. hum. genet.* 32, 53

27 Christitich, K. (1968). [Daniel Hugon is condemned to 7 years' imprisonment for the murder of a prostitute.] *Le monde*, 16 octobre, p.8, col.1.

28 Cleveland, W.W., Anas, D., Smith, G.F. (1969). Radio-ulnar synostosis, behavioural disturbance and XYY chromosomes. *Jo. pediat.*, 74, 103

29 Close, H.G., Goonetilleke, A.S.R., Jacobs, P.A. & Price, W.H. (1968). The incidence of sex chromosomal abnormalities in mentally subnormal males. *Cytogenetics*, 7, 277

30 Collier, J.G. (1966). The YY syndrome. *Lancet*, 1, 1036

31 Cornwell, J.G. & Herrmann, W. (1958). Intersexuality in mental deficient patients. *Acta endocrin.* 27, 369

32 Correra, M. (1969) I fattori biologici della criminalita: la sindrome cromosomica. *Scuola positiva*, 74, (4), 533

33 Court Brown, W.M. (1962). Sex chromosomes and the law. *Lancet*, 2, 508

34 Court Brown, W.M. (1967a). Genetics and crime. *Jo. Roy. Coll. Physicians of London*, 1, 311.

35 Court Brown, W.M. (1967b). *Human population cytogenetics*. New York: Wiley & sons

36 Court Brown, W.M. (1968a). Cytogenetic studies in humans: some population aspects. *Proc. Roy. Soc. Med.*, 61, 164

37 Court Brown, W.M. (1968b). Males with an XYY sex chromosome complement (review article). *Jo. med. genetics*, 5(4), 341

38 Court Brown, W.M. (1968c). Sex chromosome in man and its frequency with special reference to mental subnormality and criminal behaviour. *Int. rev. exper. pathol.* VII

39 Court Brown, W.M., Buckton, K.E., Jacobs, P.A., Tough, I.M., Kuenssberg, E.V. & Knox, J.D.E. (1966). Chromosome studies on adults. *Eugen. lab. monog.* 42, 1

40 Court Brown, W.M., Harnden, D.G., Jacobs, P.A., Maclean, N. & Mantle, D.J. (1964). *Abnormalities of the sex chromosome complement in man.* Special report ser. Medical Research Council, No 305. London:H.M.S.O.

41 Court Brown, W.M., Jacobs, P.A. & Price, W.H. (1968a). Sex chromosome aneuploidy and criminal behaviour. In Thoday, J.M. & Parkes, A.S. (edd.) *Genetic and environmental influence on behaviour*. Edinburgh: Oliver & Boyd.

42 Court Brown, W.M., Price, W.H. & Jacobs, P.A. (1968b). Further information on the identity of 47,XYY-males. *Brit. med. jo.*, 2, 325

43 Court Brown, W.M., Price, W.H. & Jacobs, P.A. (1968c). The XYY male.
   Brit. med. jo. 4, 513

44 Court Brown, W.M. & Smith, P.J. (1969) Human population cytogenetics.
   Brit. med. bull., 25, 74

45 Cowie, J. & Kahn, J. (1968). XYY constitution in prepubertal child.
   Brit. med. jo., 1, 748

46 Crowley, T.J. (1965). Klinefelter syndrome and abnormal behaviour: a
   case report. *Int. jo. neuropsychiatry*, 1, 359

47 Daly, R.F. (1967). The frequency and characteristic of XYY males in
   selected populations. *Amer. soc. hum. genetics abstract*, 67

48 Daly, R.F. (1969a). Mental illness and patterns of behaviour in 10 XYY
   males. *Jo. nerv. ment. dis.*, 149 (4), 318

49 DALY, R.F. (1969b). Neurological abnormalities in XYY males. *Nature*
   [Lond.], 221, 472

50 Davies, T.S. (1966). YY syndrome *Lancet*, 1, 1103

51 de la Chapelle, A. (1963). Sex chromosome abnormalities among the
   mentally defective in Finland. *Jo. ment. def. res.*, 7, 129

52 de la Chapelle, A. & Hortling, H. (1960). Frekvensen au Klinefelter's
   syndrome och gonadal dysegenesi vil oligofreni. *Nord. med.*, 63, 256

53 Dowling, R.H. & Knox, S.J. (1963) Transvestism and fertility in a
   chromosomal mosaic. *Postgrad. med. jo.*, 39, 665

54 Ellis, J.R., Miller, O.J., Penrose, L.S. & Scott, G.E.B. (1961). A
   male with XXYY chromosomes *Ann. hum. genet.*, 25, 145

55 Escoffier-Lombrotti, -. (1968). [Heredity and violence.] *Le monde*,
   16 octobre, p.8, col.3

56 Ferguson-Smith, M.A. (1958). Chromatin-positive Klinefelter's syndrome
   in a mental deficiency hospital. *Lancet*, 1, 928

57 Ferguson-Smith, M.A. (1959). The prepubertal gesticular lesion in
   chromatin positive Klinefelter syndrome as seen in mentally handi-
   capped children. *Lancet*, 1, 219

58 Ferguson-Smith, M.A. (1962). Sex chromatin anomalies in mentally
   defective individuals. *Acta cytol. Symp. on sex chromatin*, p.73

59 Forsberg, J.G., Hall, B. & Ryden, A.B.V. (1965). A case of testicular
   feminisation with chromosome mosaicism. *Acta obstet. gynec. scand.*,
   44, 491

60 Forssman, H. (1967). Epilepsy in an XYY man. *Lancet*, 1, 1389

61 Forssman, H., Akesson, H.O. & Wallin, L. (1968). The YY syndrome.
   Lancet, 2, 779

62 Forssman, H. & Hambert, G. (1963). Incidence of Klinefelter's syndrome
   among mental patients. *Lancet*, 1, 1327

63 Forssman, H. & Hambert, G. (1967). Chromosomes and antisocial behaviour.
   Excerpta crim. 7, 113

64 Fox, R.G. (1969). XYY chromosomes and crime. *Aust. & N.Z. jo. criminol.*,
   2(1), 5

65 Fox, R.G. The XYY offender: a modern myth? (Lecture delivered at

University of Toronto, Canada, 20 Nov. 1969). To be published.

66 Fraccaro, M., Davies, P., Bott, M.G. & Schutt, W. (1962). Mental deficiency and undescended testis in two males with XYY sex chromosomes.
Folia hered. path. (Milano), <u>2</u>, 211

67 Franks, R.C., Bunting, K.W. & Engel, E. (1967). Male pseudohermaphrodit-
ism with XYY sex chromosomes. *Jo. clin. endocrin.*, <u>27</u>, 1623

68 Gibson, A.L. & Martin, L. (1968). Aggression and XXYY anomaly. *Lancet*,
<u>2</u>, 870

69 Gilbert-Dreyfus, J., Sebaoun, J. & Melinsky, M. (1965). Les formes
atypiques de la maladie de Klinefelter. *Sem.Hop.*, Paris, <u>41</u>, 2832

70 Goldstein, A.S. (1967). *The insanity defense.* New Haven: Yale University
Press

71 Goldstein, J. & Katz, J. (1963). Abolish the insanity defense, - why not?
Yale law jo., <u>72</u>, 855. Repr. in Katz, J., Goldstein, J.H. &
Dershowitz, A.M., *Psychoanalysis, psychiatry and the law*, 618. New
York: Free Press.

72 Goodman, R.M., Smith, W.S. & Migeon, C.J. (1967). Sex chromosome
abnormalities. *Nature* [Lond.], <u>216</u>, 942

73 Graven, J. (1968). Existe-t-il un "chromosome du crime"? *Rev. intern. de
criminol. et de police techn.*, <u>22</u>(4), 277

74 Graven, J. (1969). Le problème de "l'anomalie chromosomique XYY" en
criminologie: aspect actuel et prospectif. *Rev. intern. de criminol.
et de police techn.*, <u>23</u>(1), 21

75 Griffiths, A.W. & Zaremba, J. (1967). Crime and sex chromosome anomalies.
Brit. med. jo., <u>4</u>, 622

76 Gustavson, K.H. & Verneholt, J. (1968). XYY syndrome in prepubertal boy.
Hereditas, <u>60</u>, 264

77 Hambert, G. (1965). Prevalence of positive sex chromatin in unselected
adult Swedish male population. *Acta genet.* (Basel), <u>15</u>, 256

78 Hambert, G. (1966). *Males with positive sex chromatin.* Report from
Psychiatric Research Centre, St Jorgen's Hospital, University of
Götenberg. Götenberg, Sweden: Scandinavian University Books

79 Hambert, G. & Forssman, H. (1964). Mental subnormality, epilepsy,
psychosis and social maladjustment in connection with the Klinefelter
syndrome. *Intern. Copenhagen congress on the scientific study of
mental retardation*; Denmark, 7-14 Aug. 1964; pp.146-50

80 Hambert, G. & Frey, T.S. (1964). The electroencephalogram in the
Klinefelter syndrome. *Acta psychiat. scand.*, <u>40</u>, 28

81 Hauschka, T.S., Hasson, J.E., Goldstein, M.N., Koepf, G.F. & Sandberg,
A.A. (1962). An XYY man with progeny indicating familial tendency to
non-disjunction. *Amer. jo. hum. genet.* <u>14</u>, 22

82 Hienz, H.A. (1969). YY syndrome forms. *Lancet*, <u>1</u>, 155

83 Hoaken, P.C.S., Clarke, M. & Breslin, M. (1964). Psychopathology in
Klinefelter syndrome. *Psychosom. med.*, <u>26</u>, 207

84 Hope, K., Philip, A.E. & Loughran, J.M. (1967). Psychological characteristics associated with XYY sex chromosome complement in a state
mental hospital. *Brit. jo. psychiat. soc. work*, <u>113</u>, 495

85 Hunter, H. (1966). YY chromosomes and Klinefelter's syndrome. *Lancet*,
<u>1</u>, 984

86 Hunter, H. (1968). Chromatin-positive and XYY boys in approved schools. *Lancet*, 1, 816

87 Hustinx, T.W.J. & van Olphen, A.H.F. (1963). An XYY chromosome pattern in a boy with Marfan's syndrome. *Genetica*, 34, 262

88 Illchmann-Christ, A. (1959). Eine Studie zum Klinefelter-Syndrom unter besondere Berucksichtigung seiner Psychopathologie. *Beitr. Sexual-forsch.*, 18, 21

89 Ismail, A.A.A., Harkness, R.A., Kirkham, K.E., Loraine, J.A., Whatmore, P.B. & Brittain, R.P. (1968). Effect of abnormal sex-chromosome complements on urinary testosterone levels. *Lancet*, 1,220

90 Israelsohn, W.J. & Taylor, A.L. (1961). Chromatin positive presumed Klinefelter's syndrome. *Brit. med. jo.* 1, 633

91 Jacobs, P.A., Brunton, M., Melville, M.M., Brittain, R.P. & McClemont, W.F. (1965). Aggressive behaviour, mental subnormality and the XYY male. *Nature* [Lond.], 208, 1351

92 Jacobs, P.A., Price, W.H., Court Brown, W.M., Brittain, R.P. & Whatmore, P.B. (1968). Chromosome studies on men in a maximum security hospital. *Ann. hum. genet.*, 31, 339

93 Karl, H.J. & Meyer, J.E. (1964). Die Sexualität beim Klinefelter Syndrom. *Kasuist. Beitr. klin. Wschr.*, 42, 1172

94 Keith, C.G. (1968). The ocular findings in the trisomy syndromes. *Proc. Roy. Soc. Med.* 61, 251

95 Kelly, S., Almy, R. & Barnard, M. (1967). Another XYY phenotype. *Nature* [Lond.], 215, 405

96 Knox, S.J. & Nevin, N.C. (1969). XYY chromosomal constitution in prison populations. *Nature* [Lond.], 222, 596

97 Kosenow, W. & Pfeiffer, R.A. (1966). YY syndrome with multiple malform-ations. *Lancet*, 1, 1375

98 Kosenow, W. & Pfeiffer, R.A. (1967). YY-syndrom. *Mschr. Kinderheilk.*, 115, 24

99 Kvale, J.N. & Fishman, J.R. (1965). The psychosocial aspects of Klinefelter's syndrome. *Jo. Amer. med. assoc.*, 193, 567

100 Lancet. (1966). Leading article: The YY syndrome. *Lancet*, 1, 583

101 Lancet (1968). An extra X chromosome. *Lancet*, 2, 1066

102 Leff, J.P. & Scott, P.D. (1968). XYY and intelligence. *Lancet*, 1, 645

103 Lehrnbecker, W. & Lucas, G.J. (1969). Disorders of brain and connective tissue in a patient with 47,XYY karyotype. *Lancet*, 2, 796

104 Ley, J. (1967). Apports possibles de la cytogénétique humaine à l'étude de la délinquance. *Rev. de droit pénal et de criminol.*, 48(3), 392

105 Lisker, R., Zenzes, M.T. & Fonesca, M.T. (1968). YY syndrome in a Mexican. *Lancet*, 2, 635

106 Little, A.J. (1968). Comparison of a matched sample of chromosome abnormalities (XYY) with genetically normal male subnormal psycho-paths. Dissertation for B.A. degree, Sheffield University Library

107 McCulloch, C. & Hunter, W.S. (1962). A search for ocular anomalies in persons with abnormal numbers of sex chromosomes. *Canadian med. assoc. jo.* 86, 14

108 Macintyre, M.N. & Stenchever, M.A. (1969). A normal XYY man. *Lancet*, 1, 680

109 McKerracher, D.W. & Street, D.R.K. (1968). Psychological aspects of a genetic syndrome (Unpublished paper)

110 Maclean, N., Mitchell, J.L., Harnden, D.G., Court Brown, W.M., Bond, J. & Mantle, D.J. (1964). Sex chromosome abnormalities in newborn babies. *Lancet*, 1, 286

111 Maclean, N., Mitchell, J.M., Harnden, D.G., Williams, J., Jacobs, P.A., Buckton, K.A., Baikie, A.G., Court Brown, W.M., McBride, J.A., Strong, J.A., Close, H.G. & Jones, D.C. (1962). A survey of sex-chromosome abnormalities among 4514 mental defectives, *Lancet*, 1, 293

112 Matthews, M.B. & Brooks, P.W. (1968). Aggression and the YY syndrome. *Lancet*, 2, 355

113 Medical Research Council. (1967). Studies on the human Y chromosome. *Annual report*, 1966-7, 1

114 Melnyk, J., Derencsenyi, A., Vanasek, F., Rucci, A.J. & Thompson, H. (1969). XYY survey in an institution for sex offenders and the mentally ill. *Nature* [Lond.], 224, Oct. 25.

115 Mendlewick, J., Wilmotte, J. & Stocquart, R. (1970). Les déterminants génétiques de la délinquance: problèmes de l'anomalie XYY. *Rev. de droit pénal et de criminol.*, 50(5), 439

116 Miller, A. & Caplan, J. (1965). Sex-role reversal following castration of a homosexual transvestite with Klinefelter's syndrome. *Canad. Psychiat. Assoc. jo.*, 10, 223

117 Mintzer, R., Pergament, E., Berlow, S. & Sato, H. (1968). The XYY syndrome. *Jo. pediat.*, 72, 572

118 Money, J. (1963). Cytogenetic and psychosexual incongruities, with a note on space-form blindness. *Amer. jo. psychiat.*, 119, 820

119 Money, J. & Pollitt, E. (1964). Cytogenetic and psychosexual ambiguity. Klinefelter's syndrome and transvestism compared. *Arch. gen. psychiat.*, 11, 589

120 Moor, Lise. (1967a). Aberrations chromosomiques portant sur les gonosomes et comportement antisocial. *Ann. intern. de criminol.*, 6(2), 459

121 Moor, Lise. (1967b). Caryotypes avec deux chromosomes Y et troubles du comportement. *Ann. médic.-psychol.*, 1, 116

122 Moorhead, P.S., Nowell, P.C., Mellman, W.J., Battips, D.M. & Hungerford, D.A. (1960). Chromosome preparations of leucocytes cultured from human peripheral blood. *Exp. cell res.*, 20, 613

123 Mosier, H.D., Scott, L.W. & Cotter, L.H. (1960a). The frequency of the positive sex-chromatin pattern in males with mental deficiency. *Pediatrics*, 25, 291

124 Mosier, H.D., Scott, L.W. & Dingham, H.F. (1960b). Sexually deviant behaviour in Klinefelter's syndrome. *Jo. pediat.*, 57, 479

125 Muckler, L.S. (1969). Chromosomes of criminals. *Science*, 163, 1145

126 Muldal, S. & Ochey, C. (1960). The "double male": a new chromosome constitution in Klinefelter's syndrome. *Lancet*, 2, 492

127 Nielsen, J. (1964). Klinefelter's syndrome and behaviour. *Lancet*, 2, 587

128 Nielsen, J. (1968a). The XYY syndrome in a mental hospital. *Brit. jo. criminol.*, 8, 186

129 Nielsen, J. (1968b). Y chromosomes in male psychiatric patients above 180m. tall. *Brit. jo. psychiat.* 114, 1589

130 Nielsen, J. (1969). Klinefelter's syndrome and the XYY syndrome. *Acta psychiat. scand.*, suppl. 209, vol. 45

131 Nielsen, J. (1970). Criminality among patients with Klinefelter's syndrome and XYY syndrome. *Scand. jo. criminal sci.*

132 Nielsen, J., Christensen, A.L., Johnsen, S.G. & Frøland, A. (1966). Psychopathology and testis histology in a patient with the XYY syndrome. *Acta med. scand.*, 180, 747

133 Nielsen, J. & Tsuboi, T. (1969). Intelligence, E.E.G., personality deviation and criminality in patients with the XYY syndrome. *Brit. jo. psychiat.*, 115, 965

134 Nielsen, J. & Tsuboi, T. (1970). Correlation between stature, character disorder and criminality. *Brit. jo. psychiat.*, 116, 145

135 Nielsen, J., Tsuboi, T., Stürup, G. & Romano, D. (1968). XYY chromosomal constitution in criminal psychopaths. *Lancet*, 2, 576

136 Nielsen, J., Tsuboi, T., Tuver, B., Jensen, J.T. & Sachs, J. (1970). Prevalence and incidence of the XYY syndrome and Klinefelter's syndrome in an institution for criminal psychopaths. *Acta psychiat. scand.*

137 Olanders, S. (1968). Excess barr bodies in mental hospitals. *Lancet*, 2, 1244

138 Pare, C.M.B. (1956). Homosexuality and chromosomal sex. *Jo. psychosom. res.*, 1, 247

139 Pasqualini, R.Q., Vidal, J. & Bur, J.E. (1957). Psychopathology of Klinefelter's syndrome. *Lancet*, 2, 164

140 Penrose, L.S. (1955). Genetics and the criminal. *Brit. jo. delinq.*, 6, 15

141 Penrose, L.S. (1964). Review of abnormalities of the sex chromosome complement in man. *Ann. hum. genet.*, 28, 199

142 Penrose, L.S. (1967). Finger print pattern and the sex chromosomes. *Lancet*, 1, 298

143 Persson, T. (1967). An XYY man and his relatives. *Jo. ment. defic. res.* 11, 239

144 Poole, E.W. & Taylor, J.M. (1970). Preferred and non-preferred E.E.G. frequency components in postcentral areas. *Electroenceph. clin. neurophysiol.* 28, 211

145 Poole, E.W., Taylor, J.M., Sowerby, J.E. & Poole, B.G. (1966). Relationship between the frequencies of E.E.G. and tremor rhythms in health and disease. *Electroenceph. clin. neurophysiol.*, 21, 617

146 Prader, A., Schneider, J., Züblin, W., Frances, J.M. & Ruedi, K. (1958). Die Haufigkeit des echten, chromatin-positiven Klinefelter-Syndromes und seine Bezeichungen zum Schwachsinn. *Schweiz. Med. Wschr.*, 88, 917

147 Price, W.H. (1968). The electrocardiogram in males with extra Y chromosomes. *Lancet*, 1, 1106

148 Price, W.H. & Fraser, G.M. (1969). Heterotopic-bone formation in two males with the 47,XYY karyotype. *Lancet*, 2, 1134

149 Price, W.H., Strong, J.A., Whatmore, P.B. & McClemont, W.P. (1966).

Criminal patients with XYY sex-chromosome complement. *Lancet,* 1, 565

150 Price, W.H. & Whatmore, P.B. (1967a). Behaviour disorders and pattern of crime among XYY males identified at a maximum security hospital. *Brit. med. jo.,* 1, 533

151 Price, W.H. & Whatmore, P.B. (1967b). Criminal behaviour and the XYY male. *Nature* [Lond.], 213, 815

152 Pritchard, M. (1962). Homosexuality and genetic sex. *Jo. ment. sci.,* 108, 616

153 Raboch, J. & Nedoma, K. (1958). Sex chromatin and sexual behaviour. *Psychosom. med.,* 20, 55

154 Rasch, W. (1959). Exhibitionistisches Verhalten bei Klinefelter-Syndrom. *Beitr. Sexualforsch.,* 18, 70

155 Ratcliffe, S.G., Stewart, A.L., Melville, M.M., Jacobs, P.A. & Keay, A.J. (1970). Chromosome studies on 3500 newborn male infants. *Lancet,* 1, 121

156 Ricci, N. & Malacarne, P. (1964). An XYY human male. *Lancet,* 2, 721

157 Richards, B.W. & Stewart, A. (1966). The YY syndrome. *Lancet,* 1, 984

158 Roebuck, J. & Atlas, R.H. (1969). Chromosomes and the criminal. *Correct. psychiat.,* 15(3), 103.

159 Rohde, R.A. (1963). Chromatin-positive Klinefelter's syndrome: clinical and cytogenetic studies. *Jo. chron. dis.,* 16, 1139

160 Rudd, B.T., Galal, O.M. & Casey, M.D. (1968). Testosterone excretion rates in normal males and males with an XYY complement. *Jo. med. genet.,* December

161 Sandberg, A.A., Ishihara, T., Crosswhite, L.H. & Koepf, G.F. (1963). XYY genotype: report of a case in a male. *New Eng. jo. med.,* 268, 585

162 Sandberg, A.A., Koepf, G.F., Ishihara, T. & Hauschka, T.S. (1961). An XYY human male. *Lancet,* 2, 488

163 Scott, P.D. & Kahn, J. (1968). An XYY patient of above average intelligence. In West, D.J. (ed.) *Psychopathic offenders,* Cambridge: Institute of criminology, pp.56-60

164 Sergovich, F. (1969). Chromosome aberrations and criminal behaviour: a brief review. *Crim. law quart.,* 11, 303

165 Sergovich, F., Valentine, G.H., Chen, A.T.L., Kinch, R.A.H. & Smouth, M.S. (1969). Chromosome aberrations in 2159 consecutive newborn babies. *New Eng. jo. med.,* 280, 851

166 Shapiro, A. & Riddler, M.A.C. (1960). The incidence of Klinefelter's syndrome in a mental deficiency hospital. *Jo. ment. def. res.,* 4, 48

167 Silance, L. (1969). Génétique et droit. *Rev. de droit pénal et de criminol.,* 49, 871

168 Slater, E. (1967). Genetics of criminals. *World med.,* March 21, p.44

169 Spencer, D.A. (1969). An unusual sex chromosome mosaicism. *Brit. jo. psychiat.,* 115, 747

170 Stenchever, M.A. & Macintyre, M.N. (1969). A normal XYY man. *Lancet,* 1, 680

171 Stewart, J.S.S., Mack, W.S., Govan, A.D.T., Ferguson-Smith, M.A. & Lennox, B. (1959). Klinefelter's syndrome: clinical and hormonal aspects. *Qu. jo. med.,* n.s., 28, 561

172 Storr, A. (1968). *Human aggression*. Harmondsworth: Penguin

173 Stumpfl, F. (1960a). Über Differenzmuster erblichen Instinktverhaltens und Defekte der personalen Struktur bei Klinefelter-Syndrom. *Wien. klin. Wschr.*, 72, 140

174 Stumpfl, F. (1960b). Personale Begegnungsstörung und sexuale Instinktunisicherheit bei Klinefelter-Syndrom. *Wien. klin. Wschr.*, 72, 360

175 Suinn, R.M. (1969). YY syndrome and sampling techniques. *Lancet*, 1, 157

176 Taylor, A.I. (1963). Sex chromatin in the newborn. *Lancet*, 1, 912

177 Telfer, M.A. *et al.* (1967-8). Diagnosis of gross chromosomal errors in institutional populations.*Pennsyl. psychiat. quart.*, winter, 3.

178 Telfer, M.A., Baker, D., Clark, G.R. & Richardson, C.E. (1968). Incidence of gross chromosomal errors among tall criminal American males. *Science*, 159, 1249

179 Thompson, H., Melnyk, J. & Hecht, F. (1967). Reproduction and meiosis in XYY. *Lancet*, 2, 831

180 Turner, B. & Jennings, A.N. (1961). Trisomy for chromosome 22. *Lancet*, 2, 49

181 Turpin, R. & Lejeune, J. (1965). *Les chromosomes humains: caractères normaux et variations pathologiques*. Paris: G. Villars.

182 Uchida, I.A., Miller, J.R. & Soltan, H.C. (1964). Dermatoglyphics associated with the XXYY chromosome complement. *Amer. jo. hum. genet.*, 16, 284

183 Uchida, I.A., Ray, M. & Duncan, B.P. (1966). 21-trisomy with an XYY sex chromosome complement. *Jo. pediat.*, 69, 295

184 Valentine, G.N. (1969). The YY chromosome complement. *Clin. pediat.* 8(6)

185 Vanasek, F., Rucci, A.J. & Thompson, H. (1969). XYY survey in an institution for sex offenders and the mentally ill. *Nature* [Lond.], 224, 369

186 Vernet, J. (1968). Cromosomi e criminalità. *Scuola positiva,* 73(4), 551

187 Verresen, H. & van den Berghe, H. (1965). 21-trisomy and XYY. *Lancet*, 1, 609

188 Veylon, R. (1969). Chromosome XYY et criminalité. *Presse médicale,* 77(9), 333

189 Vignetti, P., Capotorti, L. & Ferrante, E. (1964). XYY chromosomal constitution with genital abnormality. *Lancet*, 2, 588

190 Walzer, S., Breau, G. & Gerald, P.S. (1969). A chromosome survey of 2400 normal new-born infants. *Jo. pediat.*, 74, 438.

191 Wegmann, T.G. & Smith, D.W. (1963). Incidence of Klinefelter's syndrome among juvenile delinquents and felons. *Lancet*, 1, 274

192 Welch, J.P., Borgaonkar, D.S. & Herr, H.M. (1967). Psychopathy, mental deficiency, aggressiveness and the XYY syndrome. *Nature* [Lond.], 214, 500

193 Wiener, S. & Sutherland, G. (1968). A normal XYY man. *Lancet*, 2, 1352

194 Wiener, S., Sutherland, G. & Bartholomew, A.A. (1969). A murderer with 47,XYY and an additional autosomal abnormality. *Aust. & N.Z. jo. criminol.*, 2, 1.

195 Wiener, S., Sutherland, G., Bartholomew, A.A. & Hudson, B. (1968). XYY males in a Melbourne prison. *Lancet,* 1, 150

196 Wiesli, B. (1962). Vergleich des phenotypischen und zellkernmorphologischen Geschlechtes bei 3029 Neugeborenen. *Acta anat.* (Basel), 51, 377

197 Wilton, E. & Lever, A. (1966). The YY syndrome. *Lancet,* 1, 1156

198 Wilton, E. & Lever, A. (1967). XYY male. *S. Afr. med. jo.,* 41, 284

199 World Medicine. (1967). Crime and chromosomes. *World med.* March 7, p.13.

200 Zublin, W. (1953). Zur Psychologie des Klinefelter's Syndroms. *Acta endocr.* (Kbh.), 14, 137

201 Zuppinger, K., Engel, E., Forbes, A.P., Mantooth, L. & Claffey, J. (1967). Klinefelter's syndrome: a clinical and cytogenetic study in 24 cases. *Acta endocr.* (Kbh.), suppl. 113, pp.17, 27